Ethelinda Elliot Beers

All Quiet Along the Potomac

And Other Poems

Ethelinda Elliot Beers

All Quiet Along the Potomac
And Other Poems

ISBN/EAN: 9783744652599

Printed in Europe, USA, Canada, Australia, Japan

Cover: Foto ©Thomas Meinert / pixelio.de

More available books at **www.hansebooks.com**

All Quiet Along the Potomac,

AND

Other Poems.

BY

ETHEL LYNN BEERS.

PORTER & COATES,
PHILADELPHIA.

PREFACE.

THE poems now collected for the first time have been contributed during several years to various publications—the earlier ones to *Harper's Magazine* and *Weekly*, and most of the later ones to the *N. Y. Ledger.* Copied by other papers, with due credit given, perhaps, at first, some of them have become nameless waifs floating on the sea of print.

The poor "Picket," whose unquiet ghost refuses to remain laid "All Quiet along the Potomac," where I left him years ago, has several claimants, all with "authentic proofs of authorship," and "Which shall it Be?" reappears under various titles at regular intervals.

So I have gathered, for the friendly hands that care to hold it, this handful of white clover and daisies. I have found Life's poetry and pathos blooming beside its trodden paths and by the doorways of its homes. If some gentle heart shall find within this sheaf some treasured waif or song remembered, or if words yet unfamiliar bring to me one new friend, I have not rhymed in vain.

ETHEL LYNN BEERS.

ORANGE, June 2, 1879.

CONTENTS.

	PAGE
ALL Quiet Along the Potomac	13
On the Shores of Tennessee	15
Whisper Softly, stainless Lilies	18
Company K	19
Our Folks	21
Picking Hops	24
On Guard	25
Fire-Proof	27
Given, not Hired	29
Three Scenes in One Woman's Life	30
Midnight	32
No Name	34
Out of Style	36
The Evergreen's Moan	38
The November Garden	40
By the Cottonwood Tree	42
The Birds' Camp-meeting	45
"Svala, Svala Honom!"	47
The Moon that Shone in Paradise	48

CONTENTS.

	PAGE
Straw Paper	50
Four-leaved Clover	51
Worldly Wisdom	53
Songs under the Ice	55
A Dreamer's Tale	57
Old-fashioned Flowers	59
One Summer	60
Because a Time may Come	62
A Year-old Sorrow	63
Grandma's Christmas	65
"The Common People heard Him gladly"	66
A Seat in the City Cars	68
Noonday Rest	69
Gone to the Country	71
Life's Holidays	72
Incorrigible	74
Into our New Home	76
Scattered Roses	77
St. John's Wort	79
The Doorway of Sleep	80
Which shall it Be?	82
Baby Looking out for Me	85
The Captive Cloud	86
Human Eyes	88
Life's Soldiers	89
The Black Sheep	91

CONTENTS.

	PAGE
Holly and Mistletoe	94
The Stranger's Prayer	96
A Word to the Old Garret	97
Daisy's Good-bye to her Doll	99
Purple	101
When Jonquils Bloom	102
One to Lose, but Three to Mourn	104
Planted by the River	106
A New Friend	107
Rich and Poor	108
Who Sails with the Ship?	116
Frost-smitten	117
Floating	119
Out with the Tide	121
Lights and Shadows	123
A November Good-Night	125
On the Stairs	126
Hidden Glory	128
Hester's Jewels	130
Dominie Day	131
Weighing the Baby	134
Fair Glances	136
The Gold Nugget	138
The Carpet of Life	140
In the Fall	142
The Boys	143

	PAGE
Star-Blooms	146
Cares I have Not	147
Drifted Away	149
Until Next Summer	153
In the Night	154
A Glad To-morrow	156
The Friend in Shadow	157
One Forest-Fire	159
The Waxen Lily	161
Tracks in the Snow	163
Little Jo	165
Grannie's Test	166
Nobody Knows	168
Old School and New	170
The Baggage-Wagon	171
North Conway	173
Lady-Bug	175
Santa Claus's Mistake	177
The Fairie Fern	179
Courageous Fear	182
Gold and Crimson	184
The Sunken Island	186
"Rack-o'-Bones"	188
Don't Wake the Baby	191
Bridges	192
The Garden-Gate	194

CONTENTS.

	PAGE
The Wife's Letter	196
Tell me, Mother	198
The Lesson of a Shadow	199
Shadows of Threescore and Ten	201
Earth's Angels	202
The Ship of the Summer-time	204
The Gray Boatman	206
The Old Doorstone	208
The Sunshine's Story	210
A Day's Campaign	212
At Last	213
The Ones who are left Behind	216
The Reason Why	218
"With Care"	220
The Deacon's Trial	221
The Spirit's Journey to Dream-land	223
A Discontented Leaf	225
The Christmas Sheaf	227
A Lost Summer	228
John Gray, Junior	230
Mabel's Mission	232
A Question	234
Even Measure	236
Bloom above, and Labor under	238
A Shining Link	239
The Postman of the Air	241

CONTENTS.

	PAGE
Woman's Kingdom	242
Paris Fashions.—(War Time)	244
Over the Lake	246
Ruth and Lot	247
Beside a Fairy Fire	249
Teddy's Letter	250
Here and There	252
The Last Letter	253
The Tuberose	254
John Eliot, the Indian Apostle	256
Hymn	261
Dinners and Darns	262
The Tree of Youth	263
Attained	264
Garland or Hawser	266
The Lost Key	268
Charcoal's Story	269
Through the Mist	271
Camp-meeting Sunday at Ocean Grove	273
A Sunday Evening Beach-service at Ocean Grove	275
Better than Diamonds	277
Home from Meeting	280
The Unbidden Guest	283
Growler Grim's Dream	285
Is it Wise?	288
The Midnight Guest	289

CONTENTS.

	PAGE
Then and Now	291
Forgive Her? No, Never!	293
A Little While	295
Grandmother's Love-letter	297
My Namesake	299
The Dragon-Fly's Quest	300
Tree-top Trouble	302
The Rose of the Ring	303
Time's Triumph	306
The Daffodils never Forget	308
A Lover's Stratagem	310
In Danger	311
Hill and Shore	312
A Question	313
The Farmer's Wife	315
Off Barnegat	317
Reunited	321
A Bachelor's Bride	322
An Old Man	323
The Snow that lies Between	326
Sympathy	327
Aunt Abby's Wings	328
Going to Sleep	330
The Buried Ship	331
Baby-Love	333
The Baby's Coming	334

	PAGE
Very Early	336
The Letters that Come Not	337
The Voice of the Children's Bell	339
Hum-Bird and Bumble	340
Baby is King	342
Johnnie's Opinion of Grandmothers	344
Kitty's Cat and Mine	345
Cradle and Grave	347

EXPLANATORY NOTES............ 349

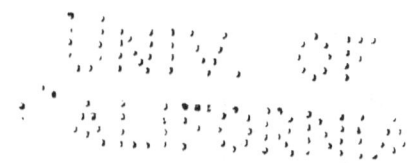

ALL QUIET ALONG THE POTOMAC.

"ALL quiet along the Potomac," they say,
  "Except, now and then, a stray picket
Is shot, as he walks on his beat to and fro,
  By a rifleman hid in the thicket.
'Tis nothing—a private or two now and then
  Will not count in the news of the battle;
Not an officer lost—only one of the men
  Moaning out, all alone, the death-rattle."

* * * * *

All quiet along the Potomac to-night,
  Where the soldiers lie peacefully dreaming;
Their tents, in the rays of the clear autumn moon
  Or the light of the watch-fire, are gleaming.
A tremulous sigh of the gentle night-wind
  Through the forest-leaves softly is creeping,
While stars up above, with their glittering eyes,
  Keep guard, for the army is sleeping.

There's only the sound of the lone sentry's tread
  As he tramps from the rock to the fountain,
And thinks of the two in the low trundle-bed
  Far away in the cot on the mountain.

His musket falls slack; his face, dark and grim,
    Grows gentle with memories tender
As he mutters a prayer for the children asleep—
    For their mother; may Heaven defend her!

The moon seems to shine just as brightly as then,
    That night when the love yet unspoken
Leaped up to his lips—when low-murmured vows
    Were pledged to be ever unbroken.
Then drawing his sleeve roughly over his eyes,
    He dashes off tears that are welling,
And gathers his gun closer up to its place,
    As if to keep down the heart-swelling.

He passes the fountain, the blasted pine tree,
    The footstep is lagging and weary;
Yet onward he goes through the broad belt of light,
    Toward the shade of the forest so dreary.
Hark! was it the night-wind that rustled the leaves?
    Was it moonlight so wondrously flashing?
It looked like a rifle—"Ha! Mary, good-bye!"
    The red life-blood is ebbing and plashing.

All quiet along the Potomac to-night,
    No sound save the rush of the river;
While soft falls the dew on the face of the dead—
    The picket's off duty for ever!

ON THE SHORES OF TENNESSEE.

"MOVE my arm-chair, faithful Pompey,
    In the sunshine bright and strong,
For this world is fading, Pompey—
    Massa won't be with you long;
And I fain would hear the south wind
    Bring once more the sound to me
Of the wavelets softly breaking
    On the shores of Tennessee.

"Mournful though the ripples murmur
    As they still the story tell,
How no vessels float the banner
    That I've loved so long and well,
I shall listen to their music,
    Dreaming that again I see
Stars and Stripes on sloop and shallop
    Sailing up the Tennessee.

"And, Pompey, while old massa's waiting
    For Death's last despatch to come,
If that exiled starry banner
    Should come proudly sailing home,
You shall greet it, slave no longer;
    Voice and hand shall both be free
That shout and point to Union colors
    On the waves of Tennessee."

"Massa's berry kind to Pompey,
    But ole darkey's happy here,

Where he's tended corn and cotton
   For dese many a long-gone year.
Over yonder missis' sleeping—
   No one tends her grave like me:
Mebbe she would miss the flowers
   She used to love in Tennessee.

"'Pears like she was watching massa;
   If Pompey should beside him stay,
Mebbe she'd remember better
   How for him she used to pray—
Telling him that 'way up yonder
   White as snow his soul would be,
Ransomed by the Lord of heaven,
   Out of life in Tennessee."

Silently the tears were rolling
   Down the poor old dusky face,
As he stepped behind his master,
   In his long-accustomed place.
Then a silence fell around them
   As they gazed on rock and tree,
Pictured in the placid waters
   Of the rolling Tennessee.

Master, dreaming of the battle
   Where he fought by Marion's side,
When he bid the haughty Tarleton
   Stoop his lordly crest of pride;
Man, remembering how yon sleeper
   Once he held upon his knee,

Ere she loved the gallant soldier,
    Ralph Vervain of Tennessee.

Still the south wind fondly lingers
    'Mid the veteran's silver hair;
Still the bondman, close beside him,
    Stands behind the old arm-chair;
With his dark-hued hand uplifted,
    Shading eyes, he bends to see
Where the woodland, boldly jutting,
    Turns aside the Tennessee.

Thus he watches; cloud-born shadows
    Glide from tree to mountain-crest,
Softly creeping, aye and ever,
    To the river's yielding breast.
Ha! above the foliage yonder,
    Something flutters wild and free!
"Massa! Massa! Hallelujah!
    The flag's come back to Tennessee!"

"Pompey, hold me on your shoulder,
    Help me stand on foot once more,
That I may salute the colors
    As they pass my cabin-door.
Here's the paper signed that frees you,—
    Give a freeman's shout with me!
'God and Union!' be our watchword
    Evermore in Tennessee!"

Then the trembling voice grew fainter,
    And the limbs refused to stand;

One prayer to Jesus—and the soldier
　Glided to that better land.
When the flag went down the river
　Man and master both were free,
While the ring-dove's note was mingled
　With the rippling Tennessee.

WHISPER SOFTLY, STAINLESS LILIES.

WHISPER softly, stainless Lilies,
　　As you fold each snowy cup
Over soldiers who are sleeping,
　With their war-tents folded up.

Bear to them our loving message,
　In thy sweet unwritten speech;
Chime, white bells, above them softly,
　Echoes only angels teach.

Tell them, Roses, as you wither,
　Tho' their dust shall heed you not;
Still by song and flag and blossom
　We would prove them unforgot.

Show them, Pansy's purple shadow,
　Through thy heart of golden bloom,
How the light of deeds heroic
　Overlies the darkened tomb.

Passion-flow'r with mystic meaning,
　Lordly, bannered Fleur-de-Lis,

Mignonette and pale Narcissus,
  Soldier dust, we give to thee.

Myrtle crown and Laurel chaplet,
  Fragrant things that bloom and die,—
These, O camp of silent sleepers!
  Over every outpost lie.

These we leave with loving message—
  Crowns, the faithful Earth will keep,
While the sacred dust of heroes
  Still she softly holds asleep.

COMPANY K.

THERE'S a cap in the closet,
  Old, tattered, and blue,
That would be little value,
  It may be, to you;
But a crown jewel-studded
  Could not buy it to-day,
With its letters of honor,
  Brave " Company K."

The head that it sheltered
  Needs shelter no more;
Dead heroes make holy
  The trifles they wore;
So a wreath better winning
  Than laurel and bay
Seems the cap of the soldier,
  Marked " Company K."

For eyes have looked steady
    Its visor beneath
O'er the work of the reaper,
    Whose harvest is Death.
Let the muster-roll meagre
    So mournfully say
How foremost in danger
    Went "Company K"—

Whose footstep unbroken
    Came up to the town,
Where rampart and bastion
    Looked fearfully down—
Who, closing up breaches,
    Yet kept on their way,
Till guns downward pointing
    Faced "Company K."

Like cameras fearful
    Stood cannon aloof,
Till the signal was given
    To strike off a proof
Of the soul of the soldier,
    To send up to Him.
(Pray God that he knew them,
    Though bloody and dim!)

Who faltered or shivered?
    Who shunned battle-smoke?
Whose fire was uncertain?
    Whose battle-line broke?

Go ask it of History
  Years from to-day,
And the record shall tell you,
  Not " Company K."

Tho' my darling is sleeping
  To-day with the dead,
And daisies and clover
  Bloom over his head,
I smile, tho' I'm crying
  As I lay it away,
That battle-worn cap
  Lettered " Company K."

OUR FOLKS.

" HI! Harry Holly! Halt! and tell
    A fellow just a thing or two;
You've had a furlough—been to see
  How all the folks in Jersey do.
It's months agone since I was there—
  I, and a bullet from Fair Oaks.
When you were home, old comrade, say,
  Did you see any of our folks?

"You did? Shake hands. Oh, ain't I glad?
  For if I do look grim and rough,
I've got some feelin'.
            People think
  A soldier's heart is mighty tough;

But, Harry, when the bullets fly,
   And hot saltpetre flames and smokes,
While whole battalions lie afield,
   One's apt to think about his folks.

"And so you saw them? When? and where?
   The old man—is he lively yet?
And mother—does she fade at all,
   Or does she seem to pine and fret
For me? And Sis—has she grown tall?
   And did you see her friend—you know
That Annie Moss?
               (How this pipe chokes!)
Where did you see her? Tell me, Hal,
   A lot of news about our folks.

"You saw them in the church, you say;
   It's likely, for they're always there."
"Not Sunday." "No? A fun'ral? Who?
   Why, Harry, how you shake and stare!
'All well,' you say, and all were out.
   What ails you, Hal? Is this a hoax?
Why don't you tell me, like a man,
   What is the matter with our folks?"

"I said all well, old comrade, true;
   I say all well, for He knows best
Who takes the young ones in his arms
   Before the sun goes to the west.
The axe-man Death deals right and left,
   And flowers fall as well as oaks;

And so—fair Annie blooms no more!
   And that's the matter with your folks.

"See, this long curl was kept for you;
   And this white blossom from her breast;
And here, your sister Bessie wrote
   A letter telling all the rest.
Bear up, old friend."
                    Nobody speaks;
   Only the old camp-raven croaks,
And soldiers whisper: "Boys, be still;
   There's some bad news from Granger's folks."

He turns his back (the only foe
   That ever saw it) on this grief,
And, as men will, keeps down the tears
   Kind Nature sends to Woe's relief.
Then answers he: "Ay, Hal, I'll try;
   But in my throat there's something chokes,
Because, you see, I've thought so long
   To count her in among our folks.

"I s'pose she must be happy now,
   But still I will keep thinking too
I could have kept all trouble off
   By being tender, kind, and true.
But maybe not.
               She's safe up there;
   And when the Hand deals other strokes,
She'll stand by heaven's gate, I know,
   And wait to welcome in our folks."

PICKING HOPS.

ON the hills of old Otsego,
    By her brightly gleaming lake,
Where the sound of horn and hunter
    Sylvan echoes love to wake,
Where the wreaths of twining verdure
    Clamber to the saplings' tops,
I sat beside sweet Minnie Wilder
    In the great field picking hops.

Then the clusters green and golden
    Binding in her sunny hair,
Half afraid, yet very earnest,
    Looking in her face so fair;
Speaking low, while Squire Von Lager
    Talked of past and coming crops,
Said I, "Minnie, should a soldier
    Stay at home here, picking hops?

"While the country, torn asunder,
    Calls for men like me to fight,
And the voice of patriots pleading
    Asks for hands to guard the right;
While from hearts of heroes slaughtered
    Still the life-blood slowly drops,
Can I—shall I stay beside you,
    Minnie darling, picking hops?"

Very pale the cheek was growing,
    And the hand I held was cold;

But the eye was bright and glowing,
  While my troubled thought was told;
Yet her voice was clear and steady,
  Without sigh, or tear, or stops,
When she answered, speaking quickly,
  " 'Tis women's work, this picking hops.

" Men should be where duty calls them—
  Women stay at home and pray
For the gallant absent soldier,
  Proud to know he would not stay."
" Bravely spoken, darling Minnie!"
  Then I kissed her golden locks,
Breathed anew a soldier's promise,
  As we sat there picking hops.

" Now I go away to-morrow,
  And I'll dare to do or die,
Win a leader's straps and sword, love,
  Or 'mid fallen heroes lie.
Then, when all of earth is fading,
  And the fluttering life-pulse stops,
Still, 'mid thoughts of home and heaven,
  I'll remember picking hops."

ON GUARD.

OPEN your eyes, my darling;
  Gather the snowy lid
Off from the sleeping glory
  Under the lashes hid.

How can I tell, my darling,
   What you would choose to say,
If the bright brown eyes were open,
   The white lid drawn away?

Never was doorway barred
   So close as the blue-veined gate;
Wake! I am here, my darling;
   I would, but I cannot, wait.

Softly the shining glory
   Lifts in the waking eyes,
And a flash like summer lightning
   Tells of a glad surprise.

Then, with a lover's craving,
   I ask of the eyes again
If their tale is true for ever,
   And find, with a jealous pain,

That behind their brightest glitter
   Lies that I cannot see,
And thoughts may crouch behind them
   That speak no word to me.

O human soul so near me,
   Still with thy visor barred,
When shall I know thee truly,
   Without thy starry guard?—

Never to read thee better,
   Never to read aright,

Till blots and blanks and errors
  The world beyond makes right?

So shut your eyes, my darling;
  My heart is beating true,
But what your soul is thinking
  I'll guess the white lids through;

And so escape the knowing
  There lies a subtle mist
Across the eyes wide open
  My loving lips have kissed.

FIRE-PROOF.

THERE'S a house burned down!
  Only, gaunt and black,
Stands the smoky shaft
  Of the chimney-stack;
And the fireplace small,
  Where we sat together,
Cannot hide us now
  From the wind and weather.
But the twilight talk
  And the childish chat
By yon blistered hearth,—
  What can burn up that?

All the tender dreams
  Over hands entwined;

All the parting words
    Of the souls now shrined;
All the faces turned
    To the firelight red—
Faces furrowed now
    By the Reaper's tread;
All the cradle-songs
    To the babies sung;
All the girlish mirth
    On its embers flung,
As a gay good-night
    Promised glad good-morrow,
And the happy sleep
    Had no waking sorrow.

Ah! the falling wall
    And the flame's hot breath
Has for these no doom—
    Has for these no death.

There's a fire-proof safe
    None can mar or make,
Where we keep them close,
    For their own dear sake.

So the house may burn,
    And the chimney fall;
In our hearts they lie,
    Safe and guarded all.

GIVEN, NOT HIRED.

WE hire the roof above our heads,
    And walls to gird us round,
The garden-walk, the drooping vine,
    The rose, and blossom-mound;
But, oh that streak of sunset sky
    Between the budding trees,
The moonlight on the little porch,—
    Whom shall we pay for these?

We have musicians too all day,
    Whose flutes we did not bring;
An oriole trills all the while,
    And saucy robins sing;
While in the bush of evergreen
    A cat-bird, gray and shy,
A solo gives. Who pays the birds
    For all these songs? Not I.

Just when the twilight turns to dusk,
    And reveries are sweet,
A piping voice, exceeding small,
    Sounds by my idle feet,
And bids me listen to its tale
    Of home and household fire—
Our cricket that we did not bring,
    The song we did not hire.

The summer wind that lifts the leaves,
    To whisper soft and low

How roses and syringas bloom,
  How sweet acacias blow,
With memories of childish hours
  In garden pathways sweet—
Who sends the south wind to my door,
  With soft, unshodden feet?

Nay, these are gifts one cannot buy,
  Nor pay in market gold;
One debt uncancelled evermore
  When cycles shall have rolled.
So, lifting up a thankful heart
  To God, who gives, I cry,
"Thou knowest, Lord, I cannot pay
  For all these things; not I."

THREE SCENES IN ONE WOMAN'S LIFE.

THE gay sun looked on a goodly show
  As the hunt swept by royal Fontainebleau;
The song was hushed which the wild bird sang,
While the sylvan sounds through the alleys rang.

There were statesmen grave, there were ladies fair,
There were knightly names such as heroes wear,
While the hand which held loyal France in check
Rested prone and gloved on a horse's neck.

But the sunshine glanced from the regal crest
To a curl wind-blown on a woman's breast,

Where the fair "Montijo" a picture stood—
Far the fairest thing in the royal wood;

And it touched her cap with its plume of snow,
Lit the golden wealth of the tress below,
Showed the hunting-suit all of courtly green,
With the royal "N" on the buttons' sheen;

Then it softly kissed, with a tender grace,
The lifted glance of her lovely face.
O maiden fair, both the bird and sun
Know a woman's heart and an empire won.

*   *   *   *

Where the mould'ring dust of the Pharaohs slept,
And the desert sand over temples crept,
Came a barge ablaze with the fleur-de-lis
To the bridal-rite of the wedded sea.

Once again the sun with his tropic stare,
Looking fondly down on her face so fair,
Underneath the folds of the banners bright,
Saw a royal form in its robe of white—

Saw the wealth and pomp of an empire shed
On the jewelled locks of Eugénie's head—
Saw the queenly wave of the snowy hand
As the courtiers bent to the burning sand.

*   *   *   *

A stripling pale and sad and worn,
From love and hope and kingdom torn,

On English soil waits wearily
The next strange page of history,
Which may be turned with bayonet,
Whose pictures are with red blood wet,
Thinking, poor boy! of struggling France;
When, lo! an idle lifted glance
Sees strangers, all in convent guise,
Pass doubtingly before his eyes.

No sunshine now. Through shadow pale,
A fugitive in hood and veil
Asks for the prince. There is a cry,
A sudden lifting of the eye,
Then folded arms and smothered speech
One lesson, old as Calv'ry, teach:
Though empires die and kingdoms fall,
Sweet mother-love outlives them all.

No crown lies on her folded hair,
But silver threads are shining there,
While merry birds sing soft and low
The song they sang in Fontainebleau.

MIDNIGHT.

OH, the solemn, silent midnight!
   Oh, the hush of sleeping things,
When the hours above the sleepers
   Softly shake their dusky wings!

Then the watchers by the dying,
  Stepping softly, whisper low,
For they've heard that waiting angels
  Best at midnight love to go.

To the eye of the All-seeing,
  Doth a cloud of souls arise
From the blackness of night-nooning
  Toward the lights of Paradise?

Oh, the solemn, silent midnight!
  When a host of baby souls
Come to tenant new-made mansions
  Far and near between the poles—

Come with wailing cry and protest,
  Dimly conscious of the strife,
Wee, unwilling, helpless tenants,
  Loath to meet the tax of life.

Oh, the solemn, silent midnight!
  When the sins the daylight kissed
Turn, and stalk like ghosts before us,
  Sure to keep unwelcome tryst.

Then the good deeds, counted giants
  In the sunshine's golden gleam,
Underneath the starry zenith
  Only shrunken pigmies seem.

Oh, the blessed, silent midnight!
  When the smoke of battle, blown

Aside a moment, shows us angels
  Nearest when we seem alone.

Faithful spirits, true and tender,
  Tethered only by the stars,
Walk far down the plains of heaven,
  To meet us at the midnight's bars.

NO NAME.

WHAT shall we call our baby, wife?
  The queer, wee mortal thing,
With battling hand and restless foot,
  And ear like midge's wing.

We'll give her chrism sweet and small,
  A word that's soft and low,
A sound to hear from lips of love
  As days of earth-life go.

Pansy, or Rose, or Daisy, dear?
  Helen, or Grace, or Fay?
We've called her "Baby" long enough;
  'Tis near her christ'ning-day.

You don't care, do you, Baby dear?
  You'll gabble, cry, and crow
If we should call you Polly Ann,
  If we but speak it low.

But by and by, my woman-child,
    For tones you love to hear
Your name shall be a fairy boat
    To bear sweet loves-notes near.

And so it shall be soft and sweet,
    As wood-bird's matin shy ;
So, sweet, I can't decide to-day—
    I'll find one by and by.

    *   *   *   *

Ice-cold, and like a waxen thing,
    The quiet sleeper lies,
With hands upfolded on its breast,
    And soul gone home to Paradise.

Its small life lived, its sheaf of tears
    Bound in a bundle small,
It folded thus its waxen hands
    At some Almighty call.

Our list'ning ear no accents caught
    No name like earth-born word ;
But still methinks an angel called
    " Baby !" and Baby heard.

OUT OF STYLE.

LADY LESTER sighed—such a well-bred sigh!—
As her daughter passed the piazza by,
Slender, and pallid, and drooping over,
Like the burdened bloom of the dewy clover,
Holding a volume, in childish wise,
Close to her eager and solemn eyes,
Till stumbling feet had betrayed their trust,
And, shuffling, stirred the unpolished dust.

"No style at all," Lady Lester spoke,
As another sigh on the silence broke.
"Not a bit of style—just her pa again;
He's a clumsy soul, though the best of men.
Straighter, Rosie! straight! hold your shoulders low!
Keep your toes turned out, and your head up—so!"

There was lifting up of the great gray eyes,
With an earnest glance, full of strange surprise
That the legend sweet of the dream-lit land
Was a vision only within her hand,
Where the princes lived only wrongs to right,
And the brownies wrought through the summer night.

"Ah! yes, mamma." With her loving smile
Rosie raised her head. For a little while
Proudly trod the path like a grenadier;
Then the story grew so exceeding queer
She forgot the charge, and the time and place,
And relapsed at once into deep disgrace.

OUT OF STYLE.

Lady Lester saw and decided then
To appeal once more to "the best of men"
Whether masters, gold, and the closest care
Could not give their Rosie "a better air."
So a new departure was planned and made,
With her soul left out of the plan they laid.

   *   *   *   *

Braces and arguments, daily walks,
Wise emulation and worldly talks,
With all the polishing tools now used,
Were thus in a wonderful system fused.

They trained her brain, in the highest school;
They trained her feet, till she stepped by rule;
They trained her tongue, till her heart was mute
Like idle walls of a soundless lute.
All through, her soul, looking out afar,
Fought underneath golden bolt and bar,
Asked higher themes for itself the while
Than new demands of the latest style.

It loved and longed for the better things
Here daily touched by the angels' wings;
From daisy buds, as they droop and nod,
To the round of stars and their hymn of God.
In dim green woods, on the sounding shore,
'Mid songs of birds, 'mid the torrent's roar,
In churchyards dim, in the sunset glow,
Through autumn winds or the winter snow,
She listened still, for she heard the while
Old-fashioned words that are out of style—

Words rarely spoken at Lester Hall,
Forgotten soon when they fell at all;
Of grand old themes—of the world to be—
Of the Open Door—and the Crystal Sea—
Or tender words that were set afloat
On the faithful air from a fisher's boat—
Of the lilies, safe in the better Care
Than the shining gems of a monarch are.—

Then the hungry soul from its harbor slipped
For a better port, and its Master shipped,
Through the Open Door to the Crystal Sea,
On the sunless light of the "time to be;"
Out of discord, pain, and misplaced endeavor,
Out of worldly care, "out of style," for ever.

Then the wounded hearts, as they saw her go,
Lighter held the earth and its shining show,
Learning all too late, as they weep to-day,
That an angel tarried, but could not stay.

THE EVERGREEN'S MOAN.

I THOUGHT, in early spring, how fair
   'Twould be to bloom for ever—
To wear my gallant Lincoln green
   Untouched by time or weather.

I saw the maples' golden gown
   About her cold feet lying,

The oak tree's dark and tattered cloak
  Off on the wild wind flying.

The crimson knots fell one by one
  Off from the rose tree's shoulder,
And so untied its robe of green
  Ere autumn nights grew colder.

The ripened grain waved me adieu;
  The bird stopped, southward going,
Then went his way. I watch alone,
  The north wind coldly blowing.

I would that I too with the rest
  Had been content to slumber;
The robe of life I coveted
  Now clothes me but to cumber.

There would have then been some regrets,
  Some whisper softly sighing,
When loit'ring lovers homeward went
  Through leaves about me dying.

And this is why to wintry winds
  I tell my thrice-told story:
Life, lonely life, when friends have gone,
  Is but a doubtful glory.

THE NOVEMBER GARDEN.

Poor old weeping, faded garden!
    Hear her moaning: "Well-a-day!
I had friends and wooing lovers
    In the merry month of May.
        Now I'm lonely,
        With me only
Lingers dark and drear decay.

"Roses, with their lips of velvet,
    Kissed me into summer's noon;
Dahlias promised faithful friendship
    'Neath the yellow harvest-moon.
        Fair and fleeting
        Was each greeting;
Kiss and promise failed me soon.

"Artemisia, scorned in summer,
    With her quaint and thrifty ways,
Only she has not forsaken
    Through the dark November days.
        But to cheer me
        Still keeps near me,
Cheerful in the white sun-rays.

"Yonder forest glows in splendor;
    Poets, artists, women fair,
Kneel before it, like an altar,
    Heavenly-lighted, blazing there,

And its glory
Gilds the story,
Tints the picture, wreathes the hair."

"O wailing, worn, forsaken garden,"
Artemisia softly said,
"Know you not there's glory waiting
When these autumn days have sped—
A sequel glory
To Life's story,
A crown of crystal for the head?"

O'er the waiting, silent garden
Came, one starry, frosty night,
Strange new robes of shining splendor,
Crystalline and strangely bright.
So morning found
The garden crowned,
And robed in mystic robe of white.

Each leaf, and bough, and carved capsule,
Seeded plume, grass-blade, and stone,
With curious screen of spiders' weaving,
In a resplendent rainbow shone.
So, ere the morn
To earth was born,
The King redeemed her for his own.

BY THE COTTONWOOD TREE.

"THEN why do I sell it?" you ask me again,
    "Big cabin an' clearin, an' all?"
Well, stranger, I'll tell you, though maybe you'll think
    It ain't any reason at all.

There's plenty of hardship in pioneer-life—
    A hard-workin' stint, at the best—
But I'd stick to it yet if it wasn't for this,
    A heart like a log in my breast.

D'ye see, over there by the cottonwood tree,
    A climbin' rose, close by a mound,
Inside of a fence made of rough cedar boughs?—
    Prairie wolves ain't too good to come round—

Well, Hetty, my darling old woman, lies there;
    Not very old either, you see;
She wa'n't more'n twenty the year we come West;
    She'd ha' been—comin' grass—thirty-three.

What a round little face an' a cheek like a peach
    She had, little Hetty, be sure!
What courage to take me! She knew all the while
    I was friendless and terrible poor.

How she worked with a will at our first little hut,
    'In the field, and among garden stuff,

Till her forehead was burned, and her poor little hand,
　Through its hardships, got rugged and rough!

But many a time, when I come in the door
　Quite sudden, I've found her just there,
With eyelids all red an' her face to the East—
　You see, all her own folks was there.

I cheered her, an' told her we'd go by and by,
　When the clearin' and ploughin' was through;
And then came the baby—he wa'n't very strong—
　So that Hetty had plenty to do.

But after a while she got gloomy again;
　She would hide in the cornfield to cry;
We hadn't no meetin' to speak of, you see,
　No woman to talk to was nigh.

An' she wanted to show little Joe to the folks;
　She was hungry, I s'pose, for the sight
Of faces she'd seen all the days of her life:
　That was nat'ral, stranger, an' right.

But just when she thought to go over the Plains
　The devils of Sioux was about;
So poor Hetty waited a harvest or two,
　Through the summer of locusts and drought.

That left us poor people. The next coming spring
　Such a wearisome fever come round;

An', stranger—hold on till I tell you; there now!—
   It laid little Joe in the ground.

I know'd then I'd got to send Hetty off East
   If I cared about keepin' her here;
She pined to a shadder, an' moped by his grave,
   Though her eyes brighter grew, and more clear.

If you'd seen her poor face when I told her I'd go
   And take her home visitin'! Well,
I'll never forget how she put out her hands
   Into mine, an', fur joy, cried a spell.

She didn't feel strong, though, that week or the next,
   An' the cough an' the fever increased;
While softly she whispered—she couldn't speak loud—
   "You'll take me by'm by, to the East?"

   *   *   *   *

She never got East; any further than that
   (And a hand pointed off to the mound);
But I'm goin' to take her and Joe, when I go,
   To her father's old buryin'-ground.

This, stranger, 's the reason I'm willin' to sell;
   You can buy at a bargain, you see;
It's mighty good land fur a settler to own,
   But it looks like a graveyard to me.

THE BIRDS' CAMP-MEETING.

DID you ever hear of the bird's camp-meeting?
  It was held the loveliest day of June;
Brother Blackbird wisely led the preaching,
  And Bob-o'-Lincoln led off each tune.

The Magpie, out on a circuit going,
  Declared himself a repentant sinner,
And then flew off and purloined a spoon
  That was lying close by a poor man's dinner.

The Parrot spoke with a claw uplifted,
  And told them a story as old as sin,
And exceeding dull; so the brethren whispered,
  And voted it an unmeaning din.

Kingfisher came from the reedy meadow,
  Piping a measure that nobody knew,
Till Robert-o'-Lincoln was quite discouraged
  Before the singer was halfway through.

A Cuckoo told, with a sound of crying,
  How slyly a Starling's nest she stole,
And that ever since she had been bemoaning
  The weary weight on her burdened soul.

Then Elder Raven his head shook sadly;
  He "hoped the bird might in earnest be;
But he didn't know; there had been confession
  So oft before this— Well, we would see."

A Redbird came in his crimson jacket,
    With silvery speeches and flowing words,
And his sermons all had exceeding power
    Among the ranks of the lady birds.

And then commenced quite a disaffection;
    Turmoil and struggle and strife ensued:
The Blackbird spoke of his accents sharply,
    And Redbird declared he was old and rude.

The Owls and Hawks with the Blackbird sided,
    The Sparrow picked at the crimson coat,
Until all the birds clamored loud together,
    Each one with his most discordant note.

Then Bob o'-Lincoln, the wise old singer,
    Resolved to conquer this threatening phase,
Proclaimed at once that the birds should mingle
    Their voices loud in a song of praise.

        *   *   *   *

Up through the fragrant forest arches,
    Afloat on breezes cloudward sent,
There rose a great, unequalled anthem
    Above the green camp-meeting tent.

And quite forgotten ere 'twas ended
    Were all the causes of complaint,
Till ugly Owl and sullen Raven
    Grew peaceful each as patient saint.

A happy thought for birds or people
    Who into hapless quarrels fall—

To leave them where they are, unsettled,
And praise the Lord who governs all.

"SVALA, SVALA HONOM!"*

NOT for thy prophetic music,
   Of the summer to be born,
Not for sake of plumage shining
   In the early April morn,
Listen I, O circling swallow,
   In the hush of twilight rest,
To thy vesper hymn so tender,
   Evening-hymn of cheer and rest:
      "Svala, svala honom!"

Since the strange unwonted twilight
   Hid the thorn-encircled Head,
Thou, O bird of consolation,
   Hast thy word of comfort said.
On the cross above Him, staying
   Wing and foot, the legend saith,
Thou, O sympathizing swallow,
   Chanted till his dying breath:
      "Svala, svala honom!"

'Tis a pretty legend truly,
   Born beneath the midnight sun,
From the monkish convent story,
   Or the painted missal won.

   * "Console, console him!"

Still I hear the echo chanted,
  Down the ages sounding sweet;
Still I hear the brooding murmur,
  Softly still thy prayer repeat:
        "Svala, svala honom!"

So I fancy cheer and comfort
  With the whirring of thy wings;
Still I wait and bid my sorrow
  Vanish when the swallow sings;
Thinking how much nearer heaven
  Birds can flutter, as they will,
Than I, and so repeat the whisper
  Through the ether blue and still:
        "Svala, svala honom!"

THE MOON THAT SHONE IN PARADISE.

O NEW old moon! O old moon new!
  Which title may I give to you?
You were not here a month ago,
  Yet here ashine to-night; and so
Conflicting statements both are true.

To-night the floods of still white rain
Come to me through the window-pane,
  Sodden with old-time memory
  Of Earth's primeval history,
When shadows were Earth's only stain.

Is this round moon, I see arise
Up its old roadway in the skies,
   Over my small horizon's rim,
   Made by the pine woods' shadow dim,
The moon that lighted Paradise?

That shone with new created beam,
O'er Eden's bright quadruple stream,
   Over the onyx pebbles going,
   Or through Havilah's gold sand flowing,
Under Euphrates' palms to gleam?

The moon that shone on Eve's bright hair,
And cloaked with light her beauty fair,
   That mirrored Eve and Paradise
   Only in kingly Adam's eyes,
Beneath a brow unlined by care?

Thy white shafts barred the dens of shade
Where harmless lions crouching laid,
   And thornless roses lifted up,
   To thee and God, each incense cup
Through silver altars, shadow frayed.

O new old moon! O new moon old!
Hast thou no tale to mortal told
   Through all these years? Nay, tell me now
   How Eden vanished, where and how
Its sinless love and sands of gold.

Tell me what lies beyond the blue,
And what the whirling star-worlds do?

Is there no jasper wall in sight,
  Whose turrets catch thy silver light,
With gates where weary souls go through?

Unanswering still, the page of white
* Circles about my hearth to-night,
  Touching the old familiar things
  Softly as angels' tender wings.
Good-night, new moon! old moon, good-night!

STRAW PAPER.*

THROUGH the thousand sounds of the summer
      noon—
Through the cricket's chirp and the robin's tune—
Through the ceaseless talk of the brook astray,
Telling leaf and stone why she came that way,

There arose a voice. It was sweet and fine,
And its tongue unknown to such ears as mine;
But the bees and the birds, and the busy things
That have nests afield, which they roof with wings,

Waited close to hear, each with bended head,
What the moaning soul of the grain-field said,
While a friendly cricket whom once I knew
Gave a free translation she vowed was true:

* Used extensively in printing.

"Tell me, gentle Earth, who hast loved me best,
Since I left the warmth of your loving breast,
Is it all of life—this, to live and die
As a creature dumb, when I fain would cry,

"As I count the days going one by one,
Knowing working moments are almost done,
While I long to do better work than now?—
Tell me, tender one, if I may, and how?"

On the brown Earth's waiting and glowing breast
Every golden head came at last to rest;
For they heard her say, "In your fall rejoice;
Through this seeming ill thou wilt find a voice:

"Through the sickle sharp, through the pounding
 flail,
Cut and beaten down, rising crushed and pale—
Through the smirch of ink, through the tramp of lead,
Shalt thou speak to men when they deem thee dead."

It was even so. When a printed word
Had the quiet pulse of a reader stirred,
She had found her voice. Like the beaten grain,
Souls are taught to speak out of depths of pain.

FOUR-LEAVED CLOVER.

"FAIR Jennie Bell, what are you seeking?
And why are you bending your head
As you slowly walk over the highway?"
"Just seeking luck-clover," she said.

"Then what will you do with it, Jennie,
    When found, the small treasure you seek?"
"Ah, a clover, four-leaved, is so lucky
    To wear with a wish for a week."

"Just beside you I spy out one nodding;"
    Her eager hands caught it with care.
I heard, I am sure, a small whisper,
    And pink flushed the forehead so fair

As she kissed the leaf, tenderly laying
    Its quadruple petals in place
In the narrow-arched sole of her slipper,
    With hopeful content on her face.

    *   *   *   *   *

The world wore its garlands of verdure,
    Its crowns, mingled roses and rue,
Many times ere I met little Jennie—
    Not "Bell" any longer, I knew.

Ah, the face had grown wan and despairing,
    The hand very slender and weak
That extended itself for the token
    I gathered, my greetings to speak.

"Did it bring you good luck, little Jennie,
    The wish of your heart, Jennie dear?"
As she stooped o'er the bunch of green leaflets
    I saw the swift shine of a tear;

And I saw, in that globule of sorrow
    (Sad lens made of pitiful rain)

Shining still on the handful of clover
  Poor Love, smitten, bleeding, and slain,

Ere she said, "When I'm resting for ever
  You'll plant these out over my bed,
And I'll find the good luck at the rootlets
  I've missed in the world overhead."

WORLDLY WISDOM.

"OH, ma, it is dreadful!
    I've quarrelled with John,
  And left him for ever,
    To live all alone.

"He will not go with me
    To party or ball;
  At home in the evening,
    He won't talk at all.

"He is perfectly horrid,
    And stingy, and queer!
  I don't want to see him,
    Or know he is near."

"Well, Tillie, I told you
    The same long ago,
  When John was beginning
    To act like a beau;

"And you might have married
    Old Gunnybag's heir.
'Tis very provoking
    For me, I declare!

"And John is a fogy,
    And acts like a brute,
To deny you a party
    Or opera suit.

"A mean ugly fellow—"
"Why, ma, I am sure
John never was stingy,
    Although he was poor.

"He is always respectful
    And clever to you—
So tender and patient
    Whatever I do!

"And now, I remember,
    He said he would go
To the Madisons' party:
    How can you talk so?

"Poor patient old fellow!
    I'm going right back;
I'll tell him I'm sorry,
    And then—I'll unpack!"

The worldly-wise mother
Looked over at me:
"I know how to manage
Matilda, you see!"

SONGS UNDER THE ICE.

ONCE the shining King of the winter frost
From the North came down, and the valley crossed,
      Stealthily creeping;
And he laughed with pride as he came to see
How the wildwood rose and the great oak tree
      Alike were sleeping.

Over empty nests in the maples hung,
Where the summer birds their songs had sung,
      Noisy and jolly;
Over stubble-fields, where the plover's call
Had piped, in tune with the waterfall,
      Notes melancholy.

Then the fir tree buttoned its dark-green coat,
With the brown cones, close to its dusky throat,
      Grim and dreary;
While the sober pine, as the sunshine paled,
To the patient side of the mountain wailed
      Its Miserere.

So the King was proud, till he came to look
At the saucy face of a laughing brook,
      Shining so merry,
Gay, as when the leaves through the summer days
Drifted to and fro, bearing errant fays
      Across their ferry.

Then he frowned and stormed, as he bid her stay;
But she louder sang, as she kept her way,
      Merry and sparkling,
Singing bars of sunshine and rests of shade,
Of the Northern brave nor the spear afraid,
      Shining and darkling.

He worked all the night by the starry gleams;
He laid a raft, made of crystal beams,
      Over rift and eddy;
And he planked it over with drifts of snow,
And he nailed it fast to the weeds below,
      Staunch and steady.

But the rebel brook sang the same old tune,
And blinked, through a flaw in the midst, at the moon,
      Slyly once or twice:
"You may chain me under and keep me fast,
But you'll hear a song as I hurry past
      Underneath the ice."

There are hidden lives in this world unseen;
You may never see through their polished sheen,
      Nor their fetters know;

But the soul chants on what it needs must say,
In its rhythm rude, in its freeborn way,
      Underneath the snow.

A DREAMER'S TALE.

IN the arm-chair in the corner,
    Half content and wholly still,
Sat I, weaving idle fancies,
    As a rhyming dreamer will—
Setting them to sombre rhythm
    As the housewife, calm and sweet,
Trod the round of daily duties
    With her brave, unfalt'ring feet.

Timidly a basement-beggar
    Knocked and asked for warmth and bread;
Then along the stair and passage
    Went the patient, steady tread.
Then I guessed the wistful glances
    Bent upon the little lad;
Well I knew the fresh remembrance
    On the face so fair and sad.

Out of this there grew a vision
    Opposite my easy-chair,
Made by idle brain and sunshine,
    Crossed with threads of daily care.

Thus I saw the gate of Glory
    Open wide, and just within
Saw my hostess, clad in garments
    Such as earth could never spin,

Full of wonder as an angel
    Held a starry circlet out,
Pointing to the jewels shining
    All the golden crown about:
"Not so many stars, O angel!
    Not so bright my risen crest!
I could do for Him so little
    When I sought to do my best."

Then the silver speech of heaven
    In my dream I plainly heard,
While the angel 'round the circle
    Told each star with loving word:
"This, O true and faithful servant,
    Is the token of thy prayer,
Crowning alms you gave the soldier,
    Who you thought would never care.

"This, the word of pity spoken
    To the outcast at your door;
This, thy whisper to the tempted,
    Bridging times of weakness o'er;
This, the good word fitly spoken
    For thine erring Christian friend;
This, thy patience under trial;
    This, thy faith firm to the end."

And then—I woke. The bar of sunshine
  Down the wall had faded quite,
And the vision with it ended
  As the shadows chased the light;
Yet I seem to hear the story,
  Seem the starry crown to see,
While the footsteps of the housewife
  Beat their rhythm patiently.

OLD-FASHIONED FLOWERS.

WHERE are the sweet old-fashioned posies,
  Quaint in form and bright in hue,
Such as grandma gave her lovers
  When she walked the garden through?

Lavender, with spikes of azure
  Pointing to the dome on high,
Telling thus whence came its color,
  Thanking with its breath the sky.

Four-o'clock, with heart upfolding,
  When the loving sun had gone,
Streak and stain of cunning crimson,
  Like the light of early dawn.

Regal lilies, many-petalled,
  Like the curling drifts of snow,
With their crown of golden anthers
  Poised on malachite below.

Morning-glories, tents of purple
  Stretched on bars of creamy white,
Folding up their satin curtains
  Inward through the dewy night.

Marigold, with coat of velvet
  Streaked with gold and yellow lace,
With its love for summer sunlight
  Written on its honest face.

Dainty pink, with feathered petals
  Tinted, curled, and deeply frayed,
With its calyx heart, half broken,
  On its leaves uplifted laid.

Can't you see them in the garden,
  Where dear grandma takes her nap?
See cherry blooms shake softly over
  Silver hair and snowy cap?

Will the modern florist's triumph
  Look so fair, or smell so sweet,
As those dear old-fashioned posies
  Blooming round our grandame's feet?

ONE SUMMER.

THE tale of the summer is ended,
  The stage-coach has passed the old mill,
The roll of the wheels echoes softly,
  Yet I by the gate linger still.

A farmer-lad, awkward and silent,
  I seem only this—nothing more—
Since a beautiful woman went yonder,
  Away by the blue mountain-door.

She seemed not to scorn my endeavor
  To ward from her roughness and harm;
The tremulous, soft little fingers
  Have tightened in trust on my arm.

. The lilies I gathered through peril
  She wore on her brow and her breast;
She, tiptoeing, leaned on my shoulder
  To peer in the robin's new nest.

Whilst I, in my sober-hued fustian,
  Wrapped soft foolish fancies and fears,
Or dreamed of a love-lighted cottage
  To crown the devotion of years.

"A friend evermore," so it ended;
  I count for "one more" on your list
Of the falcons that pull at the tether
  Enwrapping your slender white wrist.

Ah, more than yourself goeth yonder—
  Than the dream of a sweet summer lost—
Than the heart of a farmer-lad over
  The edge of that summer-time tossed.

You take the boy's trust in fair woman
  (Save his mother, God bless her for aye!);

You drag the knight's plume in the highway,
And leave it all tarnished to lie.

O beautiful, happy, lost summer!
How bitter is growing thy wine,
Distilled from the roses and lilies
That bury this lost love of mine!

BECAUSE A TIME MAY COME.

THOUGHTFUL care for worn and weary,
   Tender heart for others keep,
Lest sad mem'ry come before us
   When our loved ones lie asleep,
With their hands together folded,
   Heeding never touch of ours,
Nor kiss, nor tears, nor tender drooping
   Of beloved buds and flowers.

Leave the bitter word unspoken;
   So shalt thou be strangely glad
If there lies no backward shadow
   On dead faces wan and sad—
If a pale lip has not quivered
   For thy careless, hot reply,
And no tears for thy transgression
   Ever dimmed a lidded eye.

Soon shall come no quick forgiveness,
   As to-day, for you and me;

Though our tears and bitter wailing
  Well attest our agony.
Calm and silent, calm and silent,
  Never clod belovèd wakes,
Though remorse sits close beside it,
  And the heart repentant breaks.

Serve and wait, for when beyond us
  Lives float off to yonder shore,
Never word or loving service
  Can we render evermore.
And that river may be near us,
  In this murky light unseen,
So let us strew along its borders
  Boughs of living evergreen.

A YEAR-OLD SORROW.

A COMMON day, of sun and shade,
  To you will come the morrow;
Alas! the August clasping bears
  Date of a year-old sorrow,

That trod at first on autumn leaves,
  Then peered through Christmas holly,
Went wailing through the snow of March
  With plaintive melancholy.

It dimmed the eyes of violets,
  Cankered all summer roses,

And shivers as the harvest-moon
　　The first sad cycle closes.

A year-old sorrow!　Still it lives,
　　Moaning at midnight waking;
It wanders through the twilight gloom,
　　And weeps with daylight breaking.

It echoes in each boyish voice
　　With strange, pathetic quiver—
Such echo as the rock gives back
　　That stands across the river.

It clutches at the empty palm
　　That misses childish fingers;
It listens for a coming step,
　　And wonders why it lingers.

A year-old sorrow!　God knows best
　　How years, their round completing,
Shall hurry on, till by and by
　　Shall come that wondrous meeting,

When Sorrow's robe, all stained with tears,
　　Tattered and soiled and hoary,
Shall flutter off before the breath
　　That bursts the gate of Glory;

And Shining Ones shall tell us then
　　That pilgrim robe and fetter
Have purer kept the heavenly dress,
　　Its brightness guarded better.

GRANDMA'S CHRISTMAS.

CHRISTMAS gifts for darling grandma—
   Loving counsel we must take,
What to buy to grace her Christmas,
   What to seek, or choose, or make.

She cares not for gold and silver,
   Nor the treasures they will buy;
Silken robe and shining trinket
   Folded in their wrappings lie.

Fred shall give her fragrant flowers,
   Sprays of roses, spikes of bloom;
Lilie paint a text beloved
   To adorn her sunny room.

Hal shall pile in purple clusters,
   Grapes, the drops of summer's blood
Caught by autumn when the sunshine
   Lanced the glowing summer wood.

I must find some dainty slippers,
   Lined with fur from toe to heel,
Or a coif of something misty
   That her white hair won't conceal.

    *   *   *   *

Christmas gifts for grandma sleeping—
   Not poor gifts of human love;
Something sent by thoughtful angels
   From the Glory up above;

Not the roses freshly gathered
  That she loved on earth so well;
But the fadeless bloom of Eden,
  Amaranth and asphodel.

Not the shoes of mortal fashion
  Wait the weary, wayworn feet;
Shod with peace, they step securely
  On that shining upper street.

Not the fabric frail and misty
  Resting on the silvered hair,
But the crown He gives his children,
  Invisible, yet hovering there.

So comes grandma's Christmas morning,
  Dawning soft and silently,
Bringing God's best gifts together,
  Christ and Immortality.

"THE COMMON PEOPLE HEARD HIM GLADLY."

"THE common people heard Him gladly;"
  O tender words of life divine!
Where'er among thy blessed teachings
  Runs there a sweeter, fairer line?
The Pharisee, with captious question,
  Still doubted what He came to teach;

While watching priest and lordly Levite
   Listened, to catch Him in His speech.

The ruler over great possessions,
   Though sorrowful, came back no more ;
And kingly Herod, conscience-smitten
   For what the bloody charger bore,
Trembled within his guarded chamber,
   Lest that which bought a woman's smile
Had breathed again, and stood before him,
   With watchword won on Patmos isle.

But common folk, in sin and sorrow—
   The fisherman, with broken net ;
The hungry crowd, upon the mountain ;
   Meek Magdalen, with tresses wet ;
Sweet children, with their speech unfettered
   And unrebuked, about His knee ;
The triple household, meek and lowly,
   Whom Jesus loved at Bethany ;

The sick, the blind, the lonely widow—
   All homeless ones, in this akin,
That He too had no waiting pillow,
   No home where He might enter in,—
What wonder these, the common people,
   Should hear Him gladly, as He told
The story sweet of homes in glory,
   To them so new, to us so old !

He wore no trailing robe of splendor,
   He asked no incense-clouded rite ;

His temple was the sky above him ;
  His crown the starry one of night ;
Mingling with publicans and sinners,
  Hungry and weary by the way,
He spoke at first among the lowly
  The words whose echo lives to-day.

A SEAT IN THE CITY CARS.

FIVE o'clock !—getting late !—never mind it a bit ;
  I've a seat in the car, and here I will sit
Till my street is announced. I will, I declare !—
I have paid the half-dime—it is no more than fair.

I've been standing all day in the store and the street ;
No rest for my limbs or the soles of my feet :
I am tired to death—would not budge for a king,
For an emperor, duke, or any such thing.

If a woman comes in— Why, *they* shouldn't try
For a seat in the cars when the evening is nigh.
"Be home before sunset," I tell Rosalie
(She's a wife for a pattern ; she gets home at three).

They say, to be sure, "I can just as well stand,"
But they put up a weak little bit of a hand
In pursuit of a strap that they find is too high,
Settle down on their toes, and give up with a sigh.

Then they seem so unsteady, and waver about
When the cars with a jerk let a passenger out.
There's one getting in!—I won't look up at all,
But stare out of doors: she looks very small

Standing up in the crowd among those great men.
Her back is this way—I'll look once again.
'Tis a very nice back, and above and upon it,
With a curl peeping out, is a black velvet bonnet.

"Dear me! this is bad, then!"—Up goes the hand—
Not bigger than Rosie's—she hardly can stand.
I don't feel quite so tired; I said I'd sit still
In spite of temptations to come; and I will.

Well, I'm glad it ain't Rosie—she's not very strong;
A wee little woman, she couldn't stand long.
But stop! let me think; what if this one should be
To some other man what Rose is to me?

And how would I feel if some lazy boor
Should allow her to stand in the draft of the door?
I'm not tired a bit; I am fresh as can be—
"Here, madam, a seat." "Oh, Fred!" "Rosalie!"

NOONDAY REST.

CALMER than midnight's deepest hush
  Is the sun-bright summer nooning,
With its cloudy shadows seeking rest,
  That fall on the hill-side swooning.

Great Night with its solemn starry eyes,
    Over Day's gate asks us whither
We go—what our password is
    To the camp beyond the river.

But sunny Noon with its sleepy smile
    Ripples the grain-field over,
Without a thought of the silent graves
    That may lie beneath the clover.

Knee-deep the drowsy cattle stand
    In the water's golden glimmer,
While berry-bush and bramble-spray
    Along the hot wall shimmer.

The ploughshare glitters in the sun,
    Through murdered daisies clinging;
The nested birds leave busy bees
    To do the noonday singing.

Bright Noon no eager questions asks,
    But, like an old dame's story,
Told as she holds us on her breast,
    Croons soft of love and glory.

The weary ploughman's lazy length
    Lies in the shadow narrow
That clings about the haystack foot,
    Careless as guarded sparrow.

O peaceful hour of summer noon!
   Life has its midnight slumber;
Has it no noonday rest for us,
   When cares shall cease to cumber?

GONE TO THE COUNTRY.

GONE to the country, darling,
   Sooner than we had planned,
With a broken rosebud folded
   Softly within your hand?

What clothes took you, my darling?
   "My crimson robes made white."
Found you the path at midnight?
   "The Lamb thereon gives light."

What food upheld you fainting?
   "The Tree of Life was there."
And were you thirsty never?
   "Whoever thirsts drinks there."

And were you lonely, dearest?
   "Nay; angels round me pressed,
And Christ, my Elder Brother,
   Carried me on His breast.

"And now I've reached the country
   Where storms are all unknown;
The jasper walls are shadowless
   Around the shining throne.

"So never mind the daisies
   That on the hillside die
To give me room, or rather
   Give room for what was 'I.'

"I'll watch the crowd incoming,
   Close hov'ring by the gate;
And there, O best beloved!
   I'll sing, and praise, and wait."

LIFE'S HOLIDAYS.

HOW do they come?
   With turbulent singing,
Joy-bells gayly ringing,
Clear bugle-note calling,
Sweet flower-rain falling,
   And throbs of the drum?

When almanacs reckon,
And tell us, the morrow
Shall know not a sorrow,
That jollity reigning
Shall silence complaining,
   And come when we beckon,

What then? Cometh gladness?
Nay—through rosy robing
Comes Memory probing,

And pallid ghosts peeping,
Who should have been sleeping
Beneath sods of sadness.

But a holiday dearer
God gives us sometimes,
That needs no gay chimes,
When prayer swells to praise ;
Fair sunshiny days
That bring heaven nearer.

Glad days full of brightness,
When faces look kindly,
When friends love us blindly,
And the sunshine above us
Itself seems to love us,
And clothes us in whiteness.

Gala-days, heaven lighted,
When earth's work discloses
Not fetters, but roses ;
When winds are caressing,
And breath is a blessing,
And wrongs are all righted.

INCORRIGIBLE.

A GREAT honey-bee bustled over the lea,
    Then stopped in a field of white clover
To load up his thigh, till he scarcely could fly
    The wide sloping meadow-land over.

He sneered, as he flew, at the dragon-fly blue,
    At the swallow so airily winging,
The clear, lazy brook, droning tunes in a nook,
    The bobolink, joyfully singing.

As she went on her way, Cloverhead heard him say,
    Like a Pharisee noisily praying,
"How well it would be, if the creatures like me
    Worked always, and never were playing!

"Yon stream, with a will should be turning a mill;
    That dragon-fly, learn to make honey;
That pert bobolink, I do really think,
    If he sings, should be singing for money."

So Busy Bee sped, till he bumped his wise head
    On a cherry bough whitely in flower;
Fresh, dainty, and fair, sat a butterfly there,
    Like a queen in a summer-laid bower.

"O Butterfly gay, have you aught laid away?
    Don't you know you're a terrible sinner
To idle your time while yet in your prime,
    Having nothing laid up for your dinner?"

Fair Butterfly laughed, as a dewdrop she quaffed
  From a cherry-bloom softly unfolding:
"Good-bye, Busy Bee; don't be worrying me
  With your lectures and wearisome scolding.

"I fancy He knows that the fair ruddy rose
  For a wheat-ear was never intended;
The jewel that burns, as the humming-bird turns,
  His hand from the rainbow has blended.

"You work all the day—'tis a honey-bee's way;
  The Lord made you homely and busy;
What use would it be for a creature like me
  To be grumbling, and work myself dizzy?

"And then, don't you see, you insensible bee,
  How our world, made of fibre and feather,
Would say I was queer, stepping out of my sphere,
  Strong-minded and wrong altogether?

"I wish you no ill. You work with a will;
  But I'll swing, if I like, on a thistle,
Fan faint little flowers in odorous bowers,
  And wait for the quail's warning whistle.

"I'll sit in the sun till the summer is done;
  But long ere the cold sobbing weather
I'll pack up my clothes in the heart of a rose,
  And we'll perish like vagrants together."

INTO OUR NEW HOME.

THE hurry of the moving is over,
    And this is our bright new home,
Where never a sob has sounded,
    Where never a sin has come.

We seem to be shorter people,
    So missing our ceiling low;
The hall and the winding stairway
    Seem very long ways to go.

I stand on the threshold thinking
    Of guests we shall hither bring—
Guests who within are waiting,
    Smiling or sorrowing.

We bring it some pleasant laughter;
    Some tears, as a mortal must;
Some prayers, with our full thanksgiving;
    Some treasure that may not rust.

We'll find merry youth for Mabel;
    For Fred there is manhood's crown;
For the mother, life's sweet autumn,
    Golden, and red, and brown.

For me, as I linger longer,
    The silvery sifting snow
That comes in the truthful mirror
    As youth and its roses go.

But if, in the happy mansion
  Some shadows there be that wait,
And some that crowd in beside us,
  We fain would leave at the gate,

O Master, go in before us ;
  Be thou evermore our guest,
And then, in the sun or shadow,
  Our home with Thy smile is blest.

SCATTERED ROSES.

'TIS a pretty German story,
    Fresh as falling mountain-dews,
Told us, merely as an item,
    In the page of foreign news.

Gretchen, with her banded tresses
    Braided close like ropes of gold,
Comely skirt, and snowy kerchief
    Blossomed from the bodice fold,

Walks beside the cart of flowers,
    Dreamy, sad, and full of thought;
Thinking all the while of Gottlieb,
    Not of business, as she ought.

"Franz," the rough old dog who loved him,
    Harnessed in the shafts to draw,

Turning round to look at Gretchen,
   But a tearful visage saw.

Bright upon the bridal finger
   Shone the unaccustomed ring;
Scarcely worn ere, callèd to battle,
   Gottlieb left her sorrowing.

     *   *   *   *

Now the bitter fight is over;
   Soldier bands with flag and drum
Come marching home. But Gretchen whispers,
   "Alas! my Gottlieb does not come.

"What care I for German glory?
   One I love is lost to me;
In the trench a ghastly vision
   Of his pallid face I see.

"Ah, when strangers buy a posy,
   Calling it meantime 'Too dear,'
Do they guess the rose's dewdrop
   Is the while a woman's tear?

"Slowly, Franz! Why bound so wildly?
   Why that cry so loud and glad?
Down, I say! Alas! my flowers!
   Art wicked, Franz, or growing mad?"

     *   *   *   *

Far and wide lie scattered blossoms;
   Hark! a cry, a dog's low whine;
A dusty soldier clasping Gretchen,
   While bugles blow "Watch on the Rhine."

And passing bands go by them softly;
  Weary eyes grow moist and glad,
As, touching sleeves, the soldiers whisper,
  "The little one has found her lad."

ST. JOHN'S WORT.

IN the valleys of the Tyrol,
    When the twilight waxes dim,
And the elves are all exorcised
    By the tender vesper-hymn;

When the grim Walpurgis witches,
    Balder's host, are lying dead,—
Then they whisper tale and legend,
    Half in earnest, half in dread,

Of the dim St. John's wort shining
    Through one mystic summer night—
Of its branch across the doorway,
    Barring elfin curse and blight;

Whisper, too, a pleasant story,
    That its leaves within the shoe
Thus can make a journey tireless,
    Though its leagues be not a few.

* * *. *

If I gather from the meadow
    Slippers full to keep and wear,
Shall I never more be weary,
    Though I wander here and there?

Shall I falter on my pathway
    Never more as I do now?
Tell me then, O elfin legend,
    Where to gather, when, and how.

Must I go for it at midnight,
    When the witches gather fast?
Must I walk alone, and backward,
    Till the mystic leaf is passed?

Tell me, for I grow aweary,
    On the pathway of my life—
Weary of its sombre shadows,
    Weary of its aimless strife.

And I falter, fearful often;
    Tell me, legend, witch, or fay,
How to gather the St. John's wort,
    So I faint not by the way.

THE DOORWAY OF SLEEP.

THERE'S a strangely solemn moment
    When, outside the tent of sleep,
We lay out beyond its circle,
    All we love for God to keep.

Then, before the doorway waiting,
    Must we bid a day good-bye,

THE DOORWAY OF SLEEP.

Knowing that its shifting moments
    Crystallized for ever lie.

Then, through tangled, tattered fringes,
    Made of dreams, the soul must creep,
Ere it find the soft enrobing
    Of the fleecy folds of sleep.

Then the sentinels He gave us,
    Warders willing, strong and true,
Ask for furloughs until morning,
    That their strength they may renew,

Wearing yet both arms and armor,
    Low they lie about the door,
Pillowed on the bending poppies
    Till the dawn shall come once more.

Will they all, these loyal Senses,
    Waken at my lightest call?
Will I find that new to-morrow
    Like this vanished day at all?

Will the love I covet meet me?
    Will the health I boast be mine?
And the golden sun in heaven
    Gladden eyes that love its shine?

With a strange reluctant footstep
    Bid I world and life good-night,
Knowing never, what the morrow
    May illumine with its light.

Yet I'll trust to Him the morning,
Life and love and sense to spare,
Drop the curtain at the doorway
And pin it with a childish prayer.

WHICH SHALL IT BE?

"Which shall it be? which shall it be?"
I looked at John—John looked at me
(Dear patient John, who loves me yet
As well as tho' my locks were jet);
And when I found that I must speak,
My voice seemed strangely low and weak:
"Tell me again what Robert said;"
And then I, list'ning, bent my head.
"This is his letter:
        'I will give
A house and land while you shall live,
If, in return, from out your seven
One child to me for aye is given.'"

I looked at John's old garments worn,
I thought of all that John had borne
Of poverty and work and care,
Which I, though willing, could not share;
I thought of seven mouths to feed,
Of seven little children's need,
And then of this.
        "Come, John," said I,
"We'll choose among them as they lie

Asleep." So, walking hand in hand,
Dear John and I surveyed our band.

First to the cradle lightly stepped
Where the new nameless baby slept.
"Shall it be Baby?" whispered John.
I took his hand and hurried on
To Lily's crib. Her sleeping grasp
Held her old doll within its clasp,
Her damp curls laid like gold alight,
A glory 'gainst the pillow white.
Softly her father stooped to lay
His rough hand down in loving way,
When dream or whisper made her stir,—
Then, huskily, said John, "Not her! not her!"

We stooped beside the trundle-bed,
And one long ray of lamplight shed
Athwart the boyish faces there,
In sleep so pitiful and fair;
I saw on Jamie's rough red cheek
A tear undried. Ere John could speak,
"He's but a baby too," said I,
And kissed him as we hurried by.
Pale, patient Robbie's angel face
Still in his sleep bore suffering's trace.
"No, for a thousand crowns, not him!"
We whispered, while our eyes were dim.
Poor Dick! bad Dick! our wayward son,
Turbulent, reckless, idle one—

Could he be spared? "Nay, He who gave,
Bids us befriend him to his grave;
Only a mother's heart can be
Patient enough for such as he;
And so," said John, "I would not dare
To send him from her bedside prayer."
Then stole we softly up above,
And knelt by Mary, child of love.
"Perhaps for her 'twould better be,"
I said to John. Quite silently
He lifted up a curl astray
Across her cheek in wilful way,
And shook his head: "Nay, love, not thee!"
The while my heart beat audibly.
Only one more, our eldest lad,
Trusty and truthful, good and glad—
So like his father. "No, John, no:
I cannot, will not let him go!"

And so we wrote in courteous way
We could not give one child away;
And afterward toil lighter seemed,
Thinking of that of which we dreamed,
Happy, in truth, that not one face
We missed from its accustomed place;
Thankful to work for all the seven,
Trusting the rest to One in heaven.

BABY LOOKING OUT FOR ME.

TWO little busy hands patting on the window,
  Two laughing bright eyes looking out at me;
Two rosy red cheeks dented with a dimple;
  Mother-bird is coming; Baby, do you see?

Down by the lilac-bush, something white and azure
  Saw I in the window as I passed the tree;
Well I knew the apron and shoulder-knots of ribbon;
  All belonged to Baby, looking out for me.

    Talking low and tenderly
      To myself, as mothers will,
    Spake I softly, "God in heaven,
      Keep my darling free from ill.
    Worldly good and worldly honors
      Ask I not for her from Thee;
    But from want and sin and sorrow,
      Keep her ever pure and free."
    *   *   *   *
    Two little waxen hands
      Folded soft and silently;
    Two little curtained eyes
      Looking out no more for me;
    Two little snowy cheeks,
      Dimple-dented nevermore;
    Two little trodden shoes,
      That will never touch the floor;
    Shoulder-ribbon softly twisted,
      Apron folded, clean and white;

These are left me, and these only,
  Of the childish presence bright.

Thus He sent an answer to my earnest praying,
  Thus He keeps my darling free from earthly stain,
Thus He folds the pet lamb safe from earthly straying;
  But I miss her sadly by the window-pane.

Till I look above it; then, with purer vision,
  Sad, I weep no longer the lilac-bush to pass,
For I see her angel, pure, and white, and sinless,
  Walking with the harpers by the Sea of Glass.

   Two little snowy wings
     Softly flutter to and fro;
   Two tiny childish hands
     Beckon still to me below;
   Two tender angel eyes
     Watch me ever earnestly
   Through the loopholes of the stars;
     Baby's looking out for me.

THE CAPTIVE CLOUD.

A CLOUD crept low in the valley's breast,
  Like a weary bird in its cradle nest;
Its soft white arms round the forest flung,
Whilst its dusky feet to the streamlet clung.

When, lo! Ranger Westwind shook the leaves
And unloosed the zone of the cloudy sheaves—

THE CAPTIVE CLOUD.

Bore away, unblest by priest or charm,
The unwilling cloud on his lifted arm.

Backward the mist as it stooped was swayed,
Till its snowy robe on the crag was frayed,
And her tears were thick on the tasselled corn,
On the spider's web and the sweet hawthorn.

Heavenward going, the ravished mist
Still wept as she vanished, and softly kissed
Each living thing on the valley-side,
With the last good-bye of the mountain-bride.

The valley sighed as it saw her go
In her bridal robing of shining snow;
The streamlet muttered a troubled prayer
That his parted love might be happy there.

Upward, still upward, the soaring cloud
Drew her bridal veil like a fun'ral shroud,
Shrinking away from her bridegroom's clasp,
Till she struggled out from his stalwart grasp.

* * * * *

Then upward, still upward, she floated away
Before Heaven's court this injustice to lay;
The wind whistled shrilly to call her again,
But whistle and bluster were idle and vain.

The Lord of the winds heard the sorrowful tale,
And pitied the mourner so weary and pale;
So gave her permission, as sweet summer rain,
To kiss her old love in the valley again.

She called to a shadow, who cloaked her about
With a storm-suit of gray; but still shining out
Gleamed the hue of her robe, the scarf in her hair,
In spite of all shadowy counsel and care.

Then the Lord set his seal ('twas a radiant bow),
And bid the fair summer rain valley-ward go,
Down, down to the heart of the whispering corn,
Down, down to the stream by the blossoming thorn.

HUMAN EYES.

I GROW afraid of human eyes,
   Flashing and shining everywhere,
Holding such fearful mystery
   Of silent souls in prison there—

Afraid of that sweet, solemn thing
   That upward looks from children's eyes,
Wistfully gazing far away,
   As tho' homesick for Paradise—

Afraid of eyes, tho' fair they beam,
   Starry and dark, or bright and blue;
Crafty and cold, or soft and warm—
   All with a soul still looking through;

Peering from out each curtained gate,
   Watching beneath the eyelid's fall;
Asking, answering, quest and glance,
   Without a word or breath at all;

Leaping from quick and busy brain,
　Muscle and nerve like serfs obey,
And hasten at the spirit's call
　To gather lash and lid away,

Till by the iris' shifting shade
　It stops and looks at you and me;
An eye—a soul—or ill or good;
　Demon, or angel mystery.

Mentor or siren, friend or foe,
　The wily tongue may weave its spell;
But there outlooking stands the soul,
　A steadfast tale of truth to tell.

If Anger holds her court within,
　Or starry Hope, or bitter Woe,
Or gentle Love, or dewy Faith,
　Truth telegraphs the tidings through,

Till mortal eyes no more they seem,
　But watching soldiers, sent to stand
Between the body and the soul—
　The pickets of the Spirit Land.

LIFE'S SOLDIERS.

WITHOUT a flag of strange device
　In glowing colors bright and gay,
No nodding plume above the brow,
　Nor title blazoned U. S. A.,

They walk beside us everywhere—
   In quiet glen, in crowded street,
Wherever human hearts are borne
   About by busy human feet.

Still with their armor buckled on,
   Still fighting foes without, within,
Life's warriors walk beside us here
   To battle wrong, and war with sin.
No bugle-blast their deeds proclaims,
   No cannon booms for hero true,
Where self, and wrong, before him slain
   Proclaim the deadly conflict through.

Pale, quiet faces pass us by,
   So strangely calm we wonder still
Whence came the Lethean draught to them,
   What drops the waveless chalice fill.
The scars they bear are not from sword,
   Nor rifle-ball, nor bayonet thrust ;
They are but lines on cheek and brow,
   Engraved by broken hope and trust.

In household duties, day by day,
   Where cares and sorrows mark the round,
A feeble one may vict'ry win,
   May grasp and wear the starry crown ;
God strengthens still the weakest hand
   That grasps his weapon in His name—
Self-love subdued, hot words held back,
   A victor's wreath may win and claim.

Where toilworn hands fling back a bribe,
　　Where honesty makes good its trust,
Where promises are kept through pain,
　　Where still, tho' tempted, men are just,—
There are life's soldiers brave and true ;
　　And when this warfare shall be o'er,
As heroes brave shall those appear
　　Whose courage was undreamed before.

THE BLACK SHEEP.

FARMER GREY had a flock fair as farmer might
　　own ;
Love tended and sheltered were they ;
They trod on his toes, as the younglings will do,
　　But his heart was untrodden alway,
Till the years, rolling onward, browned brighter the
　　curls,
　　And the heads from his knee reached his shoulder ;
And then, as tho' Nature had done something odd,
　　He marvelled to find them grown older.

When fair blushing Alice and young Reuben Lee
　　Came homeward the longest way round
From school and from church, he wondered the while
　　What the children to talk about found.
Till Rose tied her hair with a twist and a curl,
　　And John trained a whisker to grow,

And Allan—the baby— Well, Allan was young,
   And boys will be wayward, you know.

      *   *   *   *

Alas, Farmer Grey! alas and alas!
   There's a stain on a lamb in the fold;
There's a sheep gone astray, a shepherd bereft,
   There's a wanderer lost in the wold.
There's a gun in the hall, and beside it a cap,
   As they were on that sunshiny day
When over the meadow and down by the mill
   Wilful Allan went off and away.

There's mother's dark eye ever glancing to see
   If there's any one turning the lane,
And when gossips ask where her youngest has gone,
   Her face flushes crimson with pain.
There's a quaver at night when the good farmer prays
   For the wandering ones everywhere;
There's a place in the Bible that opens itself
   To the promise He gives patient prayer.

O wayward black sheep over earth everywhere,
   Look back all the way you have been,
And see bleeding hearts trodden down in the way,
   And locks whiter grown for your sin—
All the way over hands for you feebly upheld,
   Over graves, over hot, bitter tears,
Till lo! flower-veiled in the bright bramble-bloom,
   Yawning black the dark pitfall appears.

      *   *   *   *

Christmas-time at the farm. Reuben Lee and his
    wife,
Fair Rose, and our grave lawyer son,
Have gathered. Moist, stealthy eyes go
    To the cap in the hall and the gun.
Farmer Grey and his wife draw nigh to the hills
    From whence the far Glory streams over,
Ere the night-shadows come and hide them a while
    Under myrtle and roses and clover.

Still mother-eyes watch, tho' their sparkle is dim,
    Still a voice for the wanderer pleads,
Tho' tremulous tones break chapter and verse,
    As the Prodigal's story he reads.
And now, as the children come back to the hearth,
    He bids them in silence draw nigh,
That, gathered again, he may give hearty thanks
    To their Master and Sovereign on high :

"God bless you, my children, and keep you His
    own !"
"And I, O my father, bless me."
Ha ! who is this soldier, with medal and strap,
    Who kneels by the patriarch's knee ?
"Thy blessing, O father ;" take home the black
    sheep,
Let it into the dear fold again,
Where the sunshine of love and the dew of thy
    prayers
Shall bid it grow white from its stain.

Then this the glad light of the holy day saw:
  Father-hands trembling raised to the sky;
Mother-arms open wide as she gathered him in
  On her dear faithful bosom to lie.
And this the clear air of the Christmas-time heard:
  "I thank Thee, great God, for this grace:
Now lettest Thy servant go home in content
  Since again I have seen the child's face."

HOLLY AND MISTLETOE.

WITH gypsy cloak and painted face,
    With elfish speech my lips between,
I stole unknown upon my friend
    To tell his fortune Hallow-e'en.

I knew how dim distrust had come
    To goad him with its angry smart;
I knew that pretty Madge, for all
    Her coquetry, was true at heart.

He only saw her smile on Fred,
    And then with frown and bitter pain
He turned away, and tried to flirt
    With rosy, golden-haired Elaine.

I saw fair Madge, behind his back,
    Grow sad and still and quite distrait,
Till Fred, discouraged, very soon
    Made some excuse, and walked away.

Above his shapely palm I bent,
  And told him, "Truly he should know
Who loved him best, at Christmas-time,
  Beneath the magic mistletoe ;

" For just when nine o'clock should strike
  A dark-eyed girl should surely stand
Beneath the Christmas bough, and bear
  A spray of holly in her hand."
        *   *   *   *
And then, as Madge's friend would do,
  I dressed at Christmas-time her hair,˙
And told her that a holly-wreath
  Would make her fairness look more fair.

I twined its coral skilfully
  Amid her braided jetty crown,
And bid her hold a little spray
  To foil her dress of golden brown.

Just when the hour of nine was nigh,
  With earnest speech and movement slow,
I walked across the room with her,
  And stopped beneath the mistletoe.
        *   *   *   *
All right ! I knew one earnest glance
  Would knit the broken bond between.
Ah, Carl, my friend, you'll never know
  What witches walk All-Hallow E'en.

THE STRANGER'S PRAYER.

THE spring wind crept through the city car,
Threading the crowded thoroughfare,
Lifting in frolic the floating curl
From the snowy throat of the laughing girl;
Turning the leaf of a reader's book,
Chasing a straw to the farthest nook;
Out at a window, in at the door,
Like a welcome guest who had been before.

It swayed the fold of the mourner's veil,
Lifting a lock from her forehead pale,
With a tender touch for the thread of gray
That had whitened there since a vanished May;
It dried a tear on her pallid cheek,
That told as plain as a tear could speak,
Without the gaze of the sombre eyes,
Of a child gone on into Paradise.

Evermore turning her glances sad
To the boyish form of a sailor-lad,
Her *vis-à-vis*, who, in day-dreams sweet,
Saw not the scenes of the busy street;
She watched the light of his flashing eye,
As blue as the tint of the summer sky;
"Some mother's darling," she said—"not mine;
'Thy will be done,' O Father! thine!"

Patient the childless mother sat,
Watching the ribbon upon his hat,

His throat-tie stirred by the idle wind,
Till a vision came to her burdened mind
Of the cruel world, and its storms to come
Ere the sailor-boy should be safe at home
From the wild Charybdis all unseen,
Where the bright "to be" is the dim "has been."

Softly, unfelt, on his forehead fair
There fell the dew of the stranger's prayer—
A lowly gift that he might not see
Till he anchors safe in Eternity.
But evermore, as the waves come in
From the sea of Life with a freight of sin,
An unseen Pilot shall be his guide
Safe through the surge of the coming tide.

Some strange constraint ever keep him back
When a danger crouches along the track;
Some star shine out over Error's brink,
When it only needs he should see, to think;
Some finger point from an angel hand,
Where roads divide, toward the better land;
Nor ever know, till he meets her there,
How much he owes to the stranger's prayer.

A WORD TO THE OLD GARRET.

YOU insensible garret!
   I thought I should see
You had changed just a little,
   As well as poor me.

But wasps at the window
  Come in as of yore,
And sunshine comes creeping
  Around by the door.

The mahogany cradle,
  With hood like a monk,
Repeats, as I rock it,
  The old-time " ka-dunk."

The books, wise and olden,
  Lean all in a row;
The sword in the rafters
  Was there long ago.

The spinning-wheel, idle,
  Crowds under the eaves;
The herbs, quaint and fragrant,
  Are hanging in sheaves.

The chest in the corner,
  Where school-books are thrown,
The maps, dim and yellow,
  The world has outgrown.

Ah! the swing in the shadow
  Is knotted up high,
Since the last little owner
  Went up to the sky.

O insensible garret!
  You don't know or care

How the children who loved you
    May wander or fare.

And yet 'tis a comfort
    To know evermore,
One spot is unchanging,
    From rafter to floor;

And there's something enduring
    We loved long ago,
Child, maiden and woman,
    From blossom to snow.

DAISY'S GOOD-BYE TO HER DOLL.

DAISY is just fifteen to-day,
    And so bequeaths her doll away,
With fine attire, to Cousin May,
        To keep for ever.

I saw her stroke the flaxen head,
And kiss the cheeks of battered red,
"Good-bye, old doll," she softly said—
        "Good-bye, for ever."

Then sad thoughts in my bosom stirred
At daughter Daisy's whispered word,
Which I unwittingly had heard,
        Remembered ever,

Far more than doll in dainty dress,
With ruddy lip and golden tress,
For Daisy passed, with that caress,
  Away for ever.

There babyhood told its last hour,
And time with strange, resistless power,
Flung off the calyx of life's flower,
  Unclosed for ever.

Ah, daughter Daisy! on the strand
Of life's bright wave I see thee stand,
While toys slip idly from thy hand,
  Shattered for ever,

Clasping new bubbles as they rise,
Grasping the bow on summer skies,
That promises to maiden eyes
  Gay tints for ever.

I, who have seen the shifting sun
Unmask cloud-pageants one by one,
See only vapors cold and dun
  Around me ever.

Yet no dark shadow will I hold,
To chill thee with its gloom and cold;
God keep thine heart from growing old,
  Now and for ever!

So let the painted plaything lie,
With but a brief and sinless sigh

PURPLE.

For babyhood passed swiftly by,
           And gone for ever,

If Daisy, laying softly down
A waxen doll in gaudy gown,
May hold her hands up for a crown
           That shines for ever.

PURPLE.

THE color-fairy in sorrow sat,
    With her brushes all awry;
Her palette, made of a tulip-leaf,
    Beside her laid, with its colors dry.

An order, straight from the Fairy Queen,
    Had come on a hum-bird's wing
For a thousand elfin parasols,
    To be finished late in spring—

Some snowy-white, some azure-ribbed,
    Some of the rose's hue;
But for the Queen the artist-elf
    Must make the color new.

Thus ran the scroll: "Red as the rose,
    Yet blue as Gentian's tender eyes;
Red as the sunset's parting glow,
    Blue as a mountain-shadow lies."

WHEN JONQUILS BLOOM.

Around the fairy's wildered head
  The morning-glories idly swung
These painted new, those folded up,
  On vine and wreath they hung,

With dainty tips of malachite,
  With ribs of red or blue,
Gay parasols for little folk—
  A thousand, lacking two.

All weary, worn, and in despair,
  The troubled fairy wept,
Till, like a tiny globe of dew,
  A tear-drop softly crept

Down from her eyes of emerald
  Over the robe she wore,
Then pattered in the red and blue
  Which still the palette bore.

Then lo! a Tyrian royal hue
  Of tears that day was born;
The Queen a purple shadow bore
  Proudly the fête-day morn.

WHEN JONQUILS BLOOM.

"WHAT shall we wear when jonquils bloom?"
  The hum of girlish chat
Came softly to the ingle nook
  Where I a dreamer, sat

Between the line of firelight flash
  And daylight's purple gloom,
Thinking how girlish voice and form
  Gladdened the dim old room.

"What will you wear, Anita, dear;
  Garnet, or friar's gray?
I mean to wear a lovely blue,
  Made in a charming way.
I'll have pink roses in my hat,
  Just perched upon the brim;
Somebody likes them—you know who;
  Not that I care for him!

"But one loves roses for themselves.
  And you—what will you wear?
Oh, if you wish a lovely shade,
  You need but match your hair.
What funny shopping that would be,
  Where fabrics, wide unrolled,
Would lack, this one the shadow brown,
  And that the gleaming gold!"

"Nay, Myrtle, I shall foil my locks,
  Not match them; so 'twill be
A pansy purple, made *en suite*,
  With basque and flounces three;
A chain of gold about my neck,
  And golden-tinted gloves, you know."
The tea-bell rang. That night—ah me!
  It seems so long ago.

For I have seen them clad for spring,
　When May blooms reddened fair;
The shadow of a mourner's veil
　Was o'er Anita's hair.
The robing of an orphan child
　Above a torn heart stirred,
And a little cry of bitter woe
　Was the weary sound I heard.

I saw sweet Myrtle white and still,
　Like a little child at rest;
No roses nodded o'er her brow,
　But lay on a stirless breast;
No azure robe about her fell,
　But white, like sunless snow.
These were the robes the maidens wore
　When jonquils ceased to blow.

ONE TO LOSE, BUT THREE TO MOURN.

ONLY one small name, graven deep in stone,
　Where the myrtle creeps o'er the churchyard sod,
Or hides itself from the beaten path
　By the faithful foot of a mourner trod.

But a mother's wail on the air goes by,
　Over myrtle stars, through the cypress tree:
"Only one I know for the grave to hold,
　And for God to keep, yet I mourn for three.

ONE TO LOSE, BUT THREE TO MOURN.

"I have lost the baby upon my breast,
  With its helpless cry, and its tiny hand
Holding fast by mine through the mighty walk
  From Babyhood into Children's Land.

"I have lost the boy, with his merry shout
  Ringing out glad songs on the shattered air,
Till its echoes fainter and finer grew
  In the vale of Youth, by its fountains fair.

"I have lost the scholar whose eager feet
  Trod careless down all the childish days,
Then, falt'ring, fell on the blossom-heap,
  With hands unclosed from its gathered bays.

"So I bow and weep o'er the single grave,
  So I take the cross that is set for me;
But a triple shadow is on the grave,
  And the heavy cross beareth branches three.

"So I try to think, as I keep my watch
  Above the sods of my darling's grave,
Should I choose, if I might, the stripling lost—
  The child I kept, or the babe He gave—

"To come down close on the river-shore,
  When I call his name from the darker brink,
Nay, this I leave to his Lord and mine,
  Content to join him by either link."

PLANTED BY THE RIVER.

HUMAN eyes never saw it,
    That seed as it fell,
Till the tears of a mourner
    Had watered it well.

No plume lifted upward
    Its fair presence told;
No blossom-touch parted
    The sombre-hued mould.

Out of sight, not forgotten
    As seasons went by,
It waited its quick'ning,
    And call from the sky,—

As safe as God's treasure,
    As sure as His word,
Till the touch of His finger
    The soul softly stirred.

And then, in sweet silence,
    It blossomed its way
Out of grasses entangled
    To sunlighted day.

What bloom-life, you ask me,
    Was hidden so long,
Yet kept unforgotten,
    Its purposes strong?

'Twas the wistful petition
Of childish saint, going
Across the dark river—
What wonder 'tis growing!

A NEW FRIEND.

I DID not know her yesterday,
This gentle friend of mine;
There was no niche unfilled, I thought,
Within this heart of mine.

To-day I know her; songs of mine
Have spoken for me while unseen,
Stretching like spider lines wind-blown
Our severed selves between.

When I have done my best she knew;
When I have failed she cared,—
Looking beyond the ink-clogged pen,
My unbreathed trials shared.

Ah! through this living type I guess
How vanished ones may keep
Some busy distaff's subtle thread
Unbroken, tho' I sleep.

And still I gladder grow to think
Some souls I do not know
As yet may meet me by and by,
And, loving me, yet tell me so.

For, after all, a critic's praise
   Or blame comes not so near
As gentle words from loving ones,
   Who hold some simple cadence dear.

For these I thank thee, busy pen,
   With point to speak, and plume to bear
My greeting to these unknown friends
   I shall know some time—here or There.

RICH AND POOR.

SUCH a terrible, tragical, heart-breaking matter
   Was brought to the ears of Miss Dynevor's
      "pater"—
So dreadful to think of, so mournful to know,
The worthy old merchant was crushed by the blow.
For Arabelle Dynevor, scarcely eighteen,
The fairest young damsel that ever was seen,
Had fallen in love (such a very bad plan!)
With a clerk of her father's—a very poor man;
And when she was asked in a roundabout way
In regard to the matter, had nothing to say,
But hung out such colors, betraying distress,
On cheek and on forehead, as seemed to confess
Some truth in the rumor.
                      So father and mother
In solemn conclave took counsel together
With Major Villait (an old family friend)
Regarding this fancy, and how it must end.

For an end it must have, and that very soon,
If they moved all this planet and joggled the moon,
To shake out the cobweb that hung in her brain,
And bring Arabella to reason again.
So Mrs. Dynevor, in lace and brocade,
Approved of the plan which the grim major laid,
Like a worldly-wise man as he was, to be sure,
To rescue the maiden from marrying poor;
And the gold-loving merchant, her father, as well
Conspired with the others against Arabelle.

A big burly ledger lay idle before
A weary young man by the counting-room door,
Who, stopping a moment, looked off and away
With a wondering thought—
                If he ever *did* play,
Or should do anything but this writing,
While other men yonder for glory were fighting,—
And then with a sigh of impatience, the fellow
Wrote down as an item the word "Arabella."
So, dropping his head on his arm as it lay,
To the region of dreams soon he floated away—
To a wonderful land where the maiden so dear
Seemed bending his whispered devotion to hear,
Now laying her hand on his hot weary brow;
Now spirited off—he never knew how—
Till swiftly the vision was shattered and broke;
And the glitter of arms through the thick battle-smoke
Blurred over the face that was sunshine to him,
And the violet eyes in the shadow grew dim.

How, shifting and fading, swift vanish away
His ledger and pen, and where they should lay
A captain's commission; beside it a steel
Gold-hilted, true-tempered—a trusty appeal.
Did he dream?
           Ay, but waking, the vision came true,
For Major Villait saw the matter quite through,
Holding up a bright picture of speedy promotion,
And a lover's reward for his patient devotion.
A whispered "good-bye," long lingering glances,
And the captain had gone to the war and its
    chances.

Then, fading, the maid lost the rose from her cheek,
And her light springing footstep grew weary and weak;
Her voice, that was once like a bird's merry song,
Was wondrously quiet the summer-day long,
Till the Dynevor mansion upon Murray Hill
Grew sad in its grandeur—so mournfully still
That a chill to the hearts of the owners there came
Lest a pale mighty hand Arabella should claim—
A bridegroom in truth rich enough in his way,
For jewels from earth he has stolen away
Which gold cannot buy from his awful domain—
Crown-jewels, reset, which shall glitter again.

So they called in the doctors of mighty repute,
Who stared in her eyes, dropping dewy and mute;
They sounded her lungs, and they counted the beat
Of her heart, lest the tide should be running too fleet,

And leave a fair wreck on the sorrowful shore
Whence oceans returning bring tidings no more.
They held up her hand, so transparent and pale,
And prescribed (just to think of it!) double-X ale.
One looked at her tongue, and discovering fever,
Declared only Hahnemann's drugs would relieve her.
Another one said, it was all indigestion,
A fault of the liver without any question.
But all shook their heads in a way quite distressing,
Her dangerous state in a manner confessing;
While poor Arabella grew paler and thinner—
Ate nothing for breakfast, the same for her dinner—
And sat looking off, with her eyes softly shining
With dew on their lids, while others were dining.

Again they resort to their counsel the major
(A family friend is a wonderful treasure),
And bid him prescribe for the heart he had smitten
While striving to win her a brilliant position.
"More going about, more life and variety,
Hither and thither—go follow society;
Buy pretty new dresses and India shawls,
And travel about to the Springs and the Falls.
Go, take my advice; ere the season is over
The girl will forget the poor soldier, her lover."
So Mrs. George Dynevor, liking the plan,
Considered the major a wonderful man,
Then bought for the damsel bright webs of the loom
As gorgeous as gardens of Persia in bloom—

Pale robes fair and soft as the summer-night mist
On the hills by the rays of the moon lightly kissed;
Rich silks trailing splendor, and camel's-hair shawls,
Gay Paris-made toilettes, for parties and balls,
With milliners' goods in the greatest variety,
Befitting a belle of our modern society,
From a seaside chapeau to an opera bonnet,
Like a wisp of cloud with a rose-shadow on it;
Scarfs, mantles, and gloves, rich jewels and laces,
For every occasion and all proper places.

They built up a wall of such trifles about her
Until Arabella in heart should grow stouter;
But ah! there was never a toilette to sigh in,
Nor one she could choose from their splendor to
    die in—
No blood-whitened robe for the city eternal,
Nor pearl of great price with its lustre supernal.

They packed up their trunks—not a small under-
    taking—
And carried the child, with her heart slowly breaking,
Away to the Springs,
              Bright fountains so healing
Where army-contractors, their new wealth revealing,
Flashed diamonds gayly in eyes that grew dimmer
For soldiers, who, dying, thus purchased that shimmer;
Where beauty and ugliness, poverty, wealth,
All stoop to the fountain for fashion or health;
Where brains tired out for a season stop thinking,
And brains never strong are diluted by drinking;

Where they play risky games—"Stakes?"
"Diamonds and hearts;"
Where they drive in calèches, coupés, and dog-carts;
But still, in the midst of the drinking and dining,
Fair, quiet, and pale, Arabella was pining.

So where the world's lovers with truest devotion
Go down to the surf of the solemn old Ocean,
There was seen on the drive the great Dynevor carriage,
And the girl who was saved from a very poor marriage.
Lord Castlemaine, fresh from the isle o'er the water,
Bent down his bald head to George Dynevor's daughter;
And Hyflyer Carbuncle said he should die
Without her (he didn't, between you and I);
A poet addressed her a wonderful sonnet;
A Quaker beau swore by the rose on her bonnet.
She cared not a whit for the heart-broken beaux—
No smile for their worship, no tear for their woes—
But, watching the moon by the sad-sounding sea,
Sat dreaming of Arthur and where he might be.

Then, finding the damsel was tired of balls,
They whirled her away to Niagara Falls,
Where, panting, she watched how the rock-shattered river
Came on to the doom that should gulf it for ever—
No rest for its flood, for its turmoil no calm,
Till the waves at its foot sung a sorrowful psalm

O'er its grave. But, so sad was the emblem it bore,
Arabella went thither to meet it no more.

Away, far away, from the Falls and the fountains,
They clambered and froze on the chilly White Mountains,
Where fat men were fain very often to stop,
And the limbs that were longest were soonest at top.
Where, lungs over-burdened, declared it a bore,
And, chary of breath, would encounter no more;
Where a stout alpen-stock proved a right trusty friend,
And weary ones wondered when climbing would end;
Till, grumbling, and panting, with scramble and hop,
They stood on the summit—the famous Tip-Top.

Looking off and away, Arabella stood gazing,
With a power of vision most truly amazing,
For all that she saw was a tent and a soldier
Beside the Potomac; and then, growing colder,
She came to her mother and asked to go home,
Like a poor little maiden too tired to roam.

  * * * * *

What arrows, sharp pointed with quivering pain,
Are the dumb printed letters in the lists of the slain!
How they bear on their shafts to the eyes up above them
Strange, solemn good-byes from soldiers who loved them!

"Dead—Captain Allaine!"
               With his face to the foe
I warrant he died. He is richer, I trow:
He owns the six feet of the earth where he lies—
Six feet of pure ether 'way up to the skies;
Six feet where the flowers shall chaplet the sod,
And daisies—bright letters designed by a God—
Shall point to the crown which our good Father keeps
For the soldier who prays ere he battles or sleeps.

Through the ranks of the wounded is walking alway
A shadowy figure robed ever in gray
(A color that's woven of darkness and light,
Like glimpses of morning through blackness of night—
An emblem of hope, who with right loving care
Sends shuttles, white-threaded, through webs of
        despair).
Unwearied, the face with its violet eyes
Still watches the soldier as wounded he lies.

But the men whisper softly, with sorrowful sighing,
"Alas! for the angel among us is dying."
The death-shadowed home that is on Murray Hill
Grows graver and sadder, more mournfully still;
The soft carpets wait for the bridegroom's still tread;
The door-bell awaits the black flag of the dead;
A sorrow is coming no riches can cure:
They have saved Arabella from marrying poor;
But with prayers and a kiss on the locks growing
        hoary,
She is going some day from their vision to glory.

WHO SAILS WITH THE SHIP?

MY shadow-craft is waiting,
    Its sails are full and white;
My ship will soon go sailing—
    Go sailing out of sight.

And who, think you, go hither?
    What cargo, rich and rare,
Lies underneath her hatches?
    What crew go hence, and where?

Well, all the ugly people
    Well known to you and me
(I do forgive them truly,
    But if they went to sea,

And in the Southern Ocean,
    Or nearing bright Cathay,
My phantom ship *should* founder,
    Its crew be cast away,

Why, there they might be happy,
    And so would you and I);
And if she were not spoken
    Would anybody cry?

All miserly curmudgeons,
    All lovers false and fair;
All parasites and idlers
    I've met with here and there;

All friends who vowed remembrance,
  And straightway then forgot;
All surly souls who envy
  The sunbeams in my lot;

All Pharisees and hard folks,
  Who count a smile a sin;
All eyes which motes discover,
  Yet bear a beam within;

Good folks who only blunder,
  Yet step on fraying strings,
Nor fear with hand unshrinking
  To touch one's holy things.

Thus is my good ship freighted.
  Does anybody know
Of any ugly people
  They think had better go?

FROST-SMITTEN.

SNOW-WHITE and cold lay the frost in the garden,
  Glittering brightly, but bitterly chill;
Snow-white and cold that morn in September,
  The ghost of the summer-time slept on the hill.

The four-o'clock shuddered and folded her petals,
  The meek mignonette bent her head;
While pale yellow leaves from the maple-tree falling
  Seemed soft silent tears for the summer-time dead.

FROST-SMITTEN.

The strawberry-vine, red flushed, lay a-dying;
   Rifled and brown stood the ranks of the corn;
And only the eye of the brave artemisia
   Looked fearlessly up in face of the morn.

     *   *   *   *   *

Snow-white and cold, tho' the roof-tree is o'er it,
   Peaceful and pallid, but bitterly chill,
There's something belovèd lies smitten for ever
   Within the white cottage just under the hill.

When trees of the forest were ripened and ready,
   When harvest had been gathered in,
When gone was the task in the quaint, pleasant
      garden,
   It was meet that his rest should begin.

So, peacefully, softly, like autumn leaves falling,
   He gave up his spirit to God;
Past threescore and ten, with locks like a snow-drift,
   We laid him down under the sod.

Now as I look from the grave by the orchard,
   I think how the frost turned to dew,
And mounted above with the souls of the flowers
   Whose forms Nature's care shall renew.

Thus looking, I try to wait calmly for morning,
   Yet wearily ever I grasp
And grope through the mists of this sorrowful
      dawning
   For a hand that my own hand can clasp.

The form that was human, wore mortal-made garments,
  That sat in the chair over there,
That hung a worn hat on a nail driven yonder,
  That spoke honest words, true and fair,—

All these clog my vision as, crying and praying,
  I read of that strange body new
In glory to rise from mortality faded,
  Exultant eternity through.

Yet vainly I try with my poor feeble powers
  To think of the loved, even there,
Without the kind smile that he wore when among us,
  Without the soft, silvery hair.

FLOATING.

IN the upward glint of the twilight flame
  I see one friend who is still the same,
Tho' he says no word nor speaks my name—

A china sailor, with resting blade
Across a blue boat lightly laid,
And a cargo fit for fairy trade.

Over the mantel-tree years agone
His cheery face like light has shone,
When sun and stars had both gone down.

It cheers me yet like bugle-note
To fancy from the tiny throat
Brave words—"Old friend, we float, we float!"

*   *   *   *   *

We *are* old friends, in truth are we;
Your boat has slept on its summer sea,
While mine has tossed most fitfully.

Your face still wears its hopeful smile:
Dream you of some bright, blooming isle,
While I grow old and sad the while?

No rocks have struck your bonny boat,
Nor winds the kerchief from your throat,
Unloosed and left astern to float.

Your cargo lies by spray unwet;
My ship has not come in as yet,
Or else off shore has been upset.

You have not tried to sound the lead,
While dark clouds scudded overhead,
Only to find the quicksand's bed.

Rest on your oar and quiet lie:
We're floating, aren't we, you and I,
Till the Pilot calls me by and by?

OUT WITH THE TIDE.

THE sailor-boy slept on his mother's breast;
    Heavily, slowly his breathing came;
And his blue eyes opened as, stooping low,
    Her soft voice whispered the sailor's name
As tho' it were sweet, while a human soul
    Still leapt at the sound of a mortal word,
To claim the familiar love-worn link
    Ere it grew in the world beyond unheard.

"Is the tide in, mother? I had a dream,
    As I tossed about through the weary night,
Of a shining boat all of purest pearl,
    And a boatman clad like the Northern Light.
He bid me sail in the pearly craft;
    And I seemed to know neither fear nor doubt
As he held me back with his shining oar,
    Saying gravely, 'Wait till the tide runs out.'

"And then I awoke. You were just asleep,
    With your poor head down on the pillow laid;
And so, as I thought of the waiting boat,
    I linked my fingers and truly prayed.
I said, 'Our Father' in earnest thrice;
    It comforts me so when I lonely bide;
But, mother dear, I am going soon—
    Going out slowly, out with the tide.

"You'll keep my shirt with the silver stars,
    Though dim with the salt sea-water now,

And tattered, because I had struggled so
  Underneath the wrecked ship's rocking prow.
You'll keep the curls that you cut away
  From off my wounded and aching head
When kindly hands brought me home to you,
  Walking as bearers with burdens tread.

"Is the tide in, mother? Ah yes, I know;
  'Tis the time for its angriest, fullest swell;
Oh, what will it carry away to sea
  Beside the sand and the little shell?
The boatman waits and the white boat rocks,
  The wet beach laughs as bubbles break,
And the wave creeps up to the solid cliff,
  Till it backward turns like a stealthy snake."

The sailor-boy closed his weary eyes,
  And turned his cheek to the loving breast,
Speaking no words, tho' his pale lips moved
  With a sorrowful moan in his troubled rest;
Until, as the morning tenderly broke,
  He kissed her softly before he died,
And the shining boatman bore him on—
  Sailing out, sailing out with the tide.

LIGHTS AND SHADOWS.

SEE! the shadows creep
Up the rocky steep,
Chasing the sunset glory;
And the river glows
Like a ruddy rose,
Telling the same old story

Of sombre night
Chasing up the light,
To the list'ning ripples merry;
'Tis the tale I hear
With a listless ear,
Crossing the Blithedale ferry.

All the sails I see
Glimmer black to me,
From the keel to the pennon flying;
Figures lined in gloom
On the sunset bloom,
Shadows on shadows lying.

See! the gulls wheel high
With a stormy cry,
They, like the sails, unlighted,
As across I go
To the shore—heigh-ho!
Is it I, or the world, benighted?
 * * * *

Now I stand once more
On the shadowed shore,
To the water slowly turning;
And I learn to-day,
In an idle way,
A lesson worth the learning.

Lo! the sails are white,
All the masts are bright,
And the ruddy flag is streaming;
Turning breasts of snow,
Wheeling sea-gulls go,
With their wide wings whitely gleaming.

So I look no more,
As I did before,
At life's shadows with repining;
If the sails are dun,
I shall know the sun
On the other side is shining.

For the gloom we see
May but brightness be
When we get across the river,
Where the sun no more
Leaves the golden shore,
And our ships are white for ever!

A NOVEMBER GOOD-NIGHT.

GOOD-NIGHT, little shivering grasses!
'Tis idle to struggle and fight
With tempest and cruel frost-fingers;
Lie down, little grasses, to-night!

The roses have gone from the garden,
And hidden their faces so fair;
The lilies have never uplifted
Since Frost found them bending in prayer.

The aster and dahlia fought bravely,
Till Ice, with his glittering crest,
A diamond dagger laid over
The bloom of each velvety breast.

The leaves of the forest lie faded,
Dry stubble is left after grain;
Yet you, little grasses, still struggle,
Still hope for the soft summer rain.

Nay, nay, even now there is weaving
Above you the fleece of the snow;
The star-pattern tracks the white shuttle
Through the loom of the storm to and fro,

Until over the moor and the mountain
'Twill lie like a thrice-blessed stole,
And the beggarly rays of November
Be made in the day-dawning whole.

Fear not for the spring-time awaking;
  'Tis sure as the path of a star ;
The Watcher unsleeping is ready
  The doorway of sleep to unbar

In time for that stir in the forest
  For the ears of a mortal too fine,
When rootlets commence their spring ploughing,
  And maple trees call up their wine.

Good-night, little shivering grasses!
  Lie down 'neath the coverlet white,
And rest till the cuckoo is singing ;
  Good-night, little grasses, good-night!

ON THE STAIRS.

THEY talked about music and fate,
  And moonlight, and swift intuition ;
They murmured of mystical lore—
  Love's advent by sweet premonition.

Then stared at the sticks of her fan
  • Till it broke—so it seems from their story—
And quoted small scraps from a song
  All about faithful love and its glory.

A compact of friendship came next,
  Like an opal, fire-hearted, soft glowing,
Till jealousy taught one the truth,
  Who woke from a dream at its showing.

And then, with the moon at the full,
　　Came a madness, a swift declaration
That Dahlia's white hand held the world
　　For her lover—the old affirmation.

She "was greatly surprised ! Did not think
　　It was earnest. So sorry—thought truly
His love was a brother's." His head
　　Swiftly whirled as she answered so coolly.

It was dark after that, for a while,
　　To the boy, who had bravely been wearing
His heart on his sleeve. A rough blow
　　Cutting deeply, like dagger unsparing.

Fifteen years ago a fair myth
　　That once touched his life very nearly
Was Dahlia. To-day at the Springs
　　The myth grew a fact very clearly.

There was, maybe, a slight quickened pulse
　　In remembrance, as some one said nigh him,
"There's Dahlia Tremaine." It was stilled
　　As a matronly figure passed by him.

Stout, blowsy, on dinners intent,
　　With dress illy-chosen and glaring ;
So Gaston saw Dahlia Tremaine,
　　The nymph of the stairway, uncaring.

Better slay pretty myths on the stairs,
  And bury them there under roses,
Lest, embodied, they shame later choice,
  When love's later blossom uncloses.

HIDDEN GLORY.

FROM Virginia's mountain-shadow
  Comes a tale of fairy-land—
Caverns hung with stony samite;
  Curtains looped with silver band;

Strange stalactites, rosy-tinted;
  Mighty chambers, deep and wide;
Fair, translucent, crystals draping
  Like the garments of a bride;

Chandelier and fretted cornice;
  Arch and groin and pillared door;
Sculptured bust and marble lily—
  Downward growth from roof to floor;

Organ-pipe, deep echoes sounding;
  Chaplets, worthy of a fay,—
These have lain unknown, unlighted,
  'Neath the hillside of Loray

Through the years, unguessed, untroubled,
  Sealèd secret in its tomb;
Leaving time for centuries
  Above the ground to bud and bloom;

While the silent grassy hillside,
   Sodding fretted roof below,
Gave no hint to hound or hunter,
   Or herdsman's footsteps to or fro.

Now, the stranger straying thither,
   Lighted by the torches' blaze,
Treads with words of whispered wonder
   All the hill-gnomes' cavern-maze.

Is it then in Gnome-land only
   Hidden beauty lies below?
Do we not some souls remember
   Whose good deeds were hidden so—

Quiet lives just close beside us,
   Treading dull and common ways,
Till through rifted earth a glory
   Shone upon the ended days?

Then we saw, resplendent, shining,
   Crystal shapes God saw the while—
The cup of water, patient vigil,
   Nightly prayer, forgiving smile,

Bridled tongue, care unacknowledged;
   Blind, we saw not day by day,
Careless as the herdsman straying
   O'er the glories of Loray.

HESTER'S JEWELS.

"IF I only were rich," I sighed softly,
   "To give to the suffering poor;
Or wise, to be teaching somebody;
   Or strong, helpful work to endure,—

"I then could show love to the Master,
   Far better than idling here now:
Being stupid, and poor, and a woman
   What work can I do, Lord, and how?"

There's Hester with basket and trowel!
   "Stop! Where are you going, my dear?"
A slight little, poorly-clad maiden
   At the call turned about and drew near.

Her small sober face dimpled over
   As she answered, "I thought I would go
To the wood for the red partridge-berries,
   And lichens, and mosses for Jo—

"Jo Campbell; you know she is failing—
   Has grown far too weary and weak
To go, as she used to each autumn,
   Her green winter-garden to seek.

"So I thought I would like to surprise her,
   And show her the Lord she loves well
Remembers her still in her weakness,
   And so sends me down to the dell.

"Good-bye." I went back to my dreaming,
　　Till sofa and firelight were not;
　Then silently rose a bright vision—
　　A crystalline, glittering grot.

　There, 'mid the crown-jewels of heaven,
　　I saw, wrought in emerald fair
　And rubies, the mosses and berries
　　That told a sick saint of God's care.

　"These are Hester's," I said very softly;
　　"These are Hester's," one echoing spake;
　And so I learned, sleeping, a lesson
　　That brought me true vision awake.

DOMINIE DAY.

WE old folks remember the day long ago
　　When our minister first trod the aisle
Through the wide, open door where the clover ablow
　　Sent its breath sweet and heavy the while.

I remember—don't you, Deacon Story?—how pale,
　　How slender and boyish he seemed,
And how as he spoke, tinting forehead and cheek,
　　Earnest blood from his heart shot and gleamed;

How after the service the elders remained,
　　And stood over there in the shade
Of the sycamores, talking about the new man,
　　And the call that should not be delayed.

I remember the fair little woman in gray
  Who, blushing in great trepidation,
Stole in at his coming one morning in May,
  To be watched by the whole congregation.

Not older than Mary—our Mary—was then;
  Only Mary is nineteen for ever,
For Time cannot touch the clay temple that's moved
  On the blest other side of the river.

I remember the two little heads as they came,
  Each nestled at first on her shoulder;
Each crowded in turn to the end of the pew
  By the next one, because he was older.

But the bride lost the roses she wore in her cheeks
  With the wearing of motherhood's crown;
A head now and then faded out of the row,
  While the rest turned from golden to brown.

And the dominie— John, did you notice to-day
  How he stooped as he passed up the aisle,
And wearily pushed the thin hair from his brow?
  "Can't he rest, John, from labor a while?

"He has prayed with the erring and counselled the weak,
  He has stood by the bed of the dying,
And borne his own sorrows, whatever they were,
  Without weak complaining and sighing.

"You and I, Deacon Story, are childless old folks,
  And the work of our hands has been blest;
Poor Dominie Day in his body and mind
  Very sadly needs comfort and rest."

Dame Story's old face brighter grew as she spoke,
  With her tremulous hand on his knee:
"For the Lord's sake—and mine, Deacon John—
  And for Mary's."
            He answered, "We'll see."

*   *   *   *   *

In the shadow of sunset sat Dominie Day
  In his study. His gray head was laid
Despairingly down on the desk where he wrote,
  And he said now and then, "I'm afraid.

"Yes, afraid of the waves, that they will overflow;
  Sore afraid for this wearied-out brain;
Afraid of the poverty coming so close.
  God help that I may not complain!"

Then he took up his cross, as a pilgrim might do
  On the road to the mountains of glory,
When just at his side stood the minister's wife
  With a missive. 'Twas from Deacon Story.

They read it quite through, and they spoke not a word,
  Tho' it gave to them comfort and rest;
A homestead for ever, a holiday month,
  A competence humble but blest.

They spoke not a word, but the dominie's hand
   Trembled down where the bright promise lay,
Then close to each other the weary ones knelt,
   And a whisper stole up, "Let us pray."

The bright evening star looking in from the west
   To the angels above told the story,
And a shining one lovingly listened, and bent
   Toward the earth from her mansion of glory.

WEIGHING THE BABY.

HOW many pounds does baby weigh—
   "Baby" who came a month ago?
How many pounds from crowning curl
   To rosy point of the restless toe?

Grandfather ties the kerchief's knot,
   Tenderly guides the swinging weight,
And over his misty glasses peers
   To read the record, "Only eight."

Softly the echo goes around;
   The father laughs at the tiny girl,
The fair young mother sings the words,
   While grandma smoothes the rumpled curl,

Stooping above the precious one,
   To fold a kiss within a prayer,
To whisper softly, "Little one,
   Grandfather did not weigh you fair."

He did not count the baby's smile,
　The love born with the helpless one;
He did not weigh the threads of care
　Of which a woman's life is spun.

No index tells the mighty worth
　Of little Baby's quiet breath,
Or heart-beat's ruddy metronome,
　Uncounted till it stops in death.

Nobody weighed the baby's soul,
　For here on earth no weights there be
That could avail. God only knows
　Its value through eternity.

Only eight pounds to hold a soul
　That seeks no angel's silver wing,
But shrines itself in human guise
　Within this fair and helpless thing.

O mother, sing your merry note!
　O father, laugh, but don't forget
From Baby's eyes looks out a soul
　To be in Eden's light reset!

FAIR GLANCES.

FAIR are all glances evermore
    From loving human eyes,
Whose silent speech we treasure up—
    Sweetest of mysteries.
From Baby's wistful questioning,
    Peering o'er being's verge,
To eyes made dim by river-mist
    Borne up by Jordan's surge.

Fair is the glance of shy surprise
    When, from the maiden's heart,
A messenger goes stealing up,
    And while the lashes part,
Holds up the love-light at the gate
    Through lid and iris fold;
Then starts away, a fearsome thing,
    Lest it might seem too bold.

Fair is the ling'ring, loving look
    The trav'ller backward sends
From the last hilltop on the way,
    Ere he that hill descends,
Back to the roof where, nested safe,
    He waited for his wings—
Back to the tree where every morn
    The well-known robin sings.

Fair is the mother's tender eye,
    Though dim its shrouded light,

When at the marriage-altar stands
  Her daughter robed in white.
Scarce trusts she one long look of love,
  Conscious the veil and ring
Have curtained off from her a shrine
  Around a crownèd king.

Fair is the feathered shaft of fire
  Shot from the lover's eye,
When, dainty, fair, and trippingly,
  The girl he loves goes by—
When brow unbends, and stern lips smile
  Beneath the beard's disguise,
For lips the tender secret keep,
  To lose it in the eyes.

But fairer far than all to see
  Is one glance God has given—
One which our Saviour sanctified
  Ere He went up to heaven—
When through His hour of agony
  He cared for Mary's woe,
And bade the tender friend He left
  A son's remêmbrance show.

It is the look a son bestows
  Upon a whitened head,
When, drawing near the wicket-gate
  With faint and falt'ring tread,

A mother bends before its arch—
   Ah, pure and sinless love,
Thine is the fairest glance of all,
   Fit for the world above!

THE GOLD NUGGET.

WHAT shining possibilities
   Of coin and link
  Glitter and blink,
  O yellow gold!
  Within thy hold,
For all thy dull humility.

Only the torment of the mill
   Has tried thy worth;
   O magic earth!
  Soon shalt thou find
  How mortal mind
Holds mastery o'er matter still.

Then out from torture hot and slow,
   From fire and wheel,
   From rasping steel,
  From rolling band,
  And cunning hand,
Thy better self shall rise and glow.

Art thou a ring, sought for a bride—
   Love's golden lock,
   Which change shall mock?

O marriage-ring!
Close, closer cling,
Tho' grief and sorrow shall betide!

Art thou a pen, whose task shall be
  To drown in ink
  What thinkers think?
  Oh, wisely write,
  That pages white
Be not the worse for ink and thee.

A clasp to hold the baby's sleeve,
  That shoulders white
  May shame the light?
  Oh, kiss the skin
  Thy links within—
Thy tracery on its whiteness leave.

A golden eagle hidden close
  In miser's clutch
  From gen'rous touch?
  O eagle, fly!
  Where misery
For thee shall hide its wants and woes.

Be worthy of thyself, O gold!
  By brain outwrought,
  By soft heart taught;
  Call charity to work with thee
  Untiringly,
And so be better than thy mould.

THE CARPET OF LIFE.

A WONDROUS web it yonder lies—
Your life or mine. Its mysteries
Of warp and woof, of light and gloom
But ape the tricks of cunning loom,
Where joys and sorrows, mingled, seem
The woven shadows of a dream—
A carpet faded and grown thin
By doors that let the wide world in.

See how the velvet leaves the thread
Beneath the world's prosaic tread,
Each careless footstep doing part
To mark the currents on this chart
Of Woman's kingdom, till they lie
Marked out to every thoughtful eye,
By tide and eddy surely left
On fleecy pile and sturdy weft.

They lie around the window's light;
They coast the mirror's shimmer bright;
Swirl from the cradle, dimly seen,
To senile arm-chair, and between
Eddy about the firelight glow;
About the chair where, soft and low,
The mother sings her hymn of rest
Over the baby on her breast.

See yonder roses faded, where
Went to and fro the steps of Care;

This corner where they still are bright,
Out of the staring common light,
With spray and leaf and bud of green,
To keep in mind the gay "has been;"
While by yon curtain-sheltered spot
Looks up the blue forget-me-not.

Perchance the carpet may not fit,
Through stress of purse or lack of wit,
And roses lie half cut in two,
As roses now and then will do—
Poor hopes that knew a moment's sun!
Ah, well! the story is not done;
Some time there'll be an upper room
Where rounded roses fair shall bloom.

Perhaps by yonder secret door
Comes wearing trouble, till the floor
Is almost seen. Let patient skill
Repair it with an earnest will;
Then there will be a spot to pray,
Where strength is needed day by day;
So best shall Life's worn carpet be
Mended with patient hand and knee.

IN THE FALL.

AWAY to the mountain, away to the fountain!
    Hie off to the hill-circled glen;
Go bathe in the billow, clasp waves for a pillow;
    The summer is on us again!
Hearts loving and tender communion surrender
    When the woods breathe their jubilant call;
"From the cities come hither, ere spring-flowers wither;"
We shall all meet again "in the fall."

There are carpets of flowers spread out in the bowers,
    Gay pictures not hung on a nail;
Soft couches of clover in meadows all over
    Bestudded with daisies so pale.
There are mirrors not gilded, but in the green builded,
    Just polished by breathings of June;
And arches so solemn, where shadow and column
    Make twilight beneath them at noon.

All softened and shaded by curtains vine-braided,
    Leaf-curtains gold shot with the sun,
In the moon's glowing splendor, when evening grows tender,
    The emerald hue fades to dun;
Then lamps, angel-lighted for pilgrims benighted,
    Are hung from the night's bending arch;
And for lullaby song, all the summer night long
    The cricket shall chirp in the larch.

Here, then, in the mountains, by strange, bitter
   fountains,
Seeking health, changing place for a whim,
We leave one another—friends, lover, and mother—
   Leave eyes that without us grow dim;
We part from them lightly, who pray for us nightly,
   Our names with a benison call;
Each merry to-morrow we drive away sorrow
   With the thought, we shall meet "in the fall."

God grant that the portal to glory immortal
   May lie through the old homestead door,
Where faces that love us may circle above us,
   To bid us good-bye nevermore!
But if 'tis denied us that loved ones beside us
   Shall gather, His hand doeth all;
And there, loving stronger, we'll wait for them
   longer,
   If we fail to meet here "in the fall."

THE BOYS.

"THE boys are coming home to-morrow!"
   Thus our rural hostess said,
Whilst Lou and I shot flitting glances
   Full of vague, unspoken dread.

Had we hither come for quiet,
   Hither fled the city's noise,

But to change it for the tumult
   Of those horrid country boys?—

Waking one with wild hallooing
   Early every summer day;
Shooting robins, teasing kittens,
   Frightening the wrens away;

Stumbling over trailing flounces;
   Thumbing volumes, gold and blue;
Clamoring for sugared dainties;
   Tracking earth the passage through.

These and other kindred trials
   Fancied we with woeful sigh.
"Those boys, those horrid boys, to-morrow!"
   Sadly whispered Lou and I.

   *   *   *   *

I wrote those lines one happy summer;
   To-day I smile to read them o'er,
Remembering how full of terror
   We watched all day the opening door.

They came—"the boys!"
                       Six feet in stature,
Graceful, easy, polished men!
   I vowed to Lou, behind my knitting,
To trust no mother's words again.

For boyhood is a thing immortal
   To every mother's heart and eye;

And sons are boys to her for ever,
   Change as they may to you and I.

To her no line comes sharply marking
   Whither or when their childhood went,
Nor when the eye-glance upward turning
   Levels, until 'tis downward bent.

Now by the window, still and sunny,
   Warmed by the rich October glow,
The dear old lady waits and watches
   Just as she waited years ago;

For Lou and I are now her daughters;
   We married "those two country boys,"
In spite of all our sad forebodings
   About their awkward ways and noise.

Lou springs up to meet a footfall;
   I list no more for coming feet;
Mother and I are waiting longer
   For steps on Beulah's golden street.

But when she blesses Lou's beloved,
   And seals it with a tender kiss,
I know that loving words go upward—
   Words to another world than this.

Always she speaks in gentle fashion
   About "my boys;" she always will,
Though one is gray, and one has vanished
   Beyond the touch of time or ill.

STAR-BLOOMS.

KING WINTER cold,
 Ere he grew old,
Repented him of murdered flowers,
 And everywhere,
 In earth and air,
Sought for the children of the showers.

 But lily pale
 In sunny vale,
Nor white anemone, saw he;
 No gentian blue,
 Nor pansy true,
Outlived his stern decree.

 Will no one bring
 The Winter King
His wish? Up spoke a wingèd wight,
 And throneward crossed:
 "I am Jack Frost,
And I will bring you blossoms bright."

 Then silently
 Above went he,
And drove a shining coulter through,
 Till all the cloud
 Was crystal-ploughed,
And snow-dust from the furrow flew.

 Soft floating down
 On Winter's crown,

Fell snow-flakes, like the blooms which died;
    Tiny and pale,
    Petalled and frail,
White flowers for a fairy bride.

    But loyal still
    To heavenly will,
They wore its signet from afar,
    For radiant whorl
    And shattered pearl
Each bore the likeness of a star.

    So saints should go
    On earth below,
Working their Master's holy will;
    Yet, firm impressed
    On brow and breast,
The Master's seal should glitter still.

CARES I HAVE NOT.

I HAVE my cares. In every lot
  We find their faces sad;
But when I count those I have not
  My very heart grows glad.

What if I must be up betimes
  To open budding flow'rs,
Or wake the birds (alas! I fear
  They would keep wretched hours)?

What if I held the quivering warp
   Of life throughout Broadway;
Must keep each single thread from harm
   Where countless shuttles play;

Must blindly guide the shifting woof
   With only mortal sight,
Which sees the wrong side of the work,
   Never on earth, the right?

What if I had the care of eyes,
   To keep them winking true,
So mote, with freight of agony,
   Their guards could ne'er go through?

What if there had been left to me
   The beating of one heart,
From tiny throbs of baby-life
   Till soul from flesh should part?

What if it were my daily work
   To keep all shadows right—
To shorten them at fervid noon,
   And lay them up at night,

So that the tiniest blade of grass
   Might not neglected be,
But have its slender shadow too,
   As well as cloud or tree?

What if I had the solemn care
   Of all the shining stars,

To drop them softly one by one
   Through morning's golden bars;

Or all along the lonely shore
   To plight faith to the tide,
And keep old Ocean's swelling pulse
   True beating, far and wide?

O God! I thank Thee that I may
   Such cares trust all to Thee,
Who watches all Thy hand has made,
   As tireless as eternity.

DRIFTED AWAY.

TO-DAY Luke is coming, and I must be here,
   His best, truest friend, as they say,
To speak solemn tidings as well as I can
   Of his wife who has drifted away.
I'll try to speak softly of her who is gone,
   Nor let the old memory wake
Of the past, when the heart I would die to have won
   Bessie took from me only to break.

Travel-worn, bearded, and brown with the sun,
   I see him come quickly more near;
God help me to tell him!
                        "My wife?   Bessie Lee?
   Can you tell me if Bessie is here?"

The little bird sings in the blossoming vine
    By the brookside that lies in our way;
I gather a flower and fling on the stream,
    And the bird twitters, "Drifted away."

A quick, troubled glance, a hand on my arm,
    A whisper hoarse:
                      "Tell me—not dead?"
"Not dead, for you see I am looking straight down,
    Not up to the sky overhead.
My friend, they have left me to tell you the tale.
    For Bessie unceasingly pray;
Luke Lee, she was lonely, and only a child
    When you left, and she drifted away.

"Away and away, like a lily afloat,
    Untethered by guidance or care—
Away and away, past warning and truth,
    Past honor, and promise, and prayer—
Away and away, past altar and hearth,
    Till it bloomed by the cross nevermore—
Away and away, till the tide of the street
    Flung it off on the pitiless shore."

I have told him, poor Luke! I turn me aside,
    Nor look on his sorrowful face;
With a slow, dragging step he has staggered away;
    He came with a boy's bounding pace.
A handkerchief, twisted and knotted and torn,
    By the brookside, is all that I see

To tell me that Luke has been here and is gone,
   While yet sings the bird in the tree.

   *   *   *   *

None knew where he went as the years rolled away,
   And we heard not the sound of his name,
While only in whispers the story was told
   Of Bessie—her weakness and shame.
Still, pitiful sorrow for youth gone astray,
   And sighs for the desolate hearth,
Were mingled with prayers for poor Bessie and Luke,
   Who might meet nevermore on the earth.

But one August night, when the low, gibbous moon
   Shot fitful gleams hither and thither,
There came up a shout from a fisherman's boat
   Just launched on the black, flowing river;
A traveller passing stopped short at the cry,
   For he heard the rude fisherman say,
"Help, master, at once! a woman's white dress
   Over yonder seems drifting away."

Ashore, still ashore, like a lily afloat,
   Untethered by guidance or care—
Ashore, still ashore, came the face wan and white,
   With its water-soaked tresses of hair—
Ashore, still ashore, till the waif from the wave
   At last on the river-bank lay,
And the traveller, Luke, from the current at last
   Drew Bessie, who drifted away.

Not dead, for a feeble and pitiful moan
    There came as the moments wore on,
And great-hearted Luke held her close to his breast,
    Like a gift from the dark waters won.
She lingered to tell him with penitent breath
    How she longed just to see him once more,
Yet dared not come home, so in wicked despair
    She bid the waves drift her ashore.

There, kneeling beside her, we prayed for her soul,
    Until, trembling yet hoping, at last
She came to the Saviour who Magdalene judged,
    And, praying, her worn spirit passed.
Till then on her lips Luke printed no kiss,
    But over the poor pallid clay
He stooped to her face, yet shed not a tear,
    As he did when she drifted away.

    *   *   *   *

That was long years ago, and I am his wife—
    Good Luke, who is tender and true—
Yet still as we walk by the blossoming vine,
    Or the little bird carols anew,
I see him grow sad, and I know very well,
    Evermore till his last dying day,
How the pain will come back at the sound of her name,
    The poor lily that drifted away.

UNTIL NEXT SUMMER.

FOLD up the robes which the summer has kissed,
    Lay them away, they will not be missed;
Crumple the furbelows fleecy and light,
Crush down the gossamer floating and white;
Fold them up softly, sweet maiden, to-day,
For the sunshine of summer has melted away.

The roses and lilies, so fair and so frail,
Have gone from the garden and died in the vale,
And pansies and gentian and sweet mignonette,
With the tears of November are drooping and wet;
So, fair little maiden, the light tissues fold
Ere the sun of December shines whitely and cold.

But dream not to wear them again, as to-day,
When the wheels of the year crush the blossoms of
    May;
For ah! the gay bodice may clasp in the breast
A heart full of sorrow and weary unrest;
And sombre-hued sackcloth the spirit may shroud,
While the form bears the colors it flaunted unbowed.

So, folding thy vesture to lay out of sight,
With sweet-smelling posies, with heart bounding
    light,
Yet fling in a prayer for the strength you may need—
A prayer which He grants to the storm-beaten reed,
For strength in its weakness, a stay evermore—
Until winters and summers on earth shall be o'er.

IN THE NIGHT.

HOW the Unseen gathers round us,
    With its voiceless whisper low,
When the deep and silent darkness
    Bids us seek ourselves to know—
Whence we are, and whither going
    When this soul shall take its flight,
Why this mystery and terror,
    Why these whispers in the night!

When we fold aside our vesture,
    Do our souls, unrobing too,
Closer come to themes immortal,
    Seeking there communion true?
Looking thus, with clearer vision,
    Toward a ray of heavenly light,
Do our spirits soar, untrammelled
    By our bodies, in the night?

Silently the stars above us
    To the zenith come and pass;
Silently the dew of heaven
    Leaves its crystals on the grass;
Silently the pale moon's crescent,
    Dropping low, sinks out of sight;
And alone with God and darkness
    We are thinking in the night—

Thinking much of mortal treasures
    Which we may have lost or won,

IN THE NIGHT.

Of our deeds for good or evil
   Ill performed, or quickly done,
While the past holds up a curtain
   Full of pictures, dark or bright,
And the future, dimly shadows
   Cloudy visions in the night.

Yet when thoughts like these are ended,
   And our wand'ring hour is past,
Comes the solemn question ever,
   "Whither shall we go at last?"
Till we fancy wistful faces,
   Bending figures all in white,
From the home of the immortals
   Beckon to us in the night.

And they whisper, " We are waiting;
   Come to us, for we to you
Can go no more, tho' earth were Eden,
   And its fleeting pleasures true."
But the gulf that lies between us
   Fills our mortal frames with fright,
And we tremble, tho' the angels
   Bend to meet us in the night.

Blessed Saviour! calm and peaceful,
   Then Thy mortal form we see;
Tho' King and Priest with crown and ephod,
   Yet lowly man of Galilee;

Bridging with thy cross the chasm,
   Quite too deep for human sight,
Thou hast taught us what to answer
   To these whispers in the night.

A GLAD TO-MORROW.

"Weeping may endure for a night, but joy cometh in the morning."

WHAT if the world has spun agee,
   Or seemed agee, since dawning,
Lay down thy head upon thy bed,
   Trusting to God and morning.

If daily toil seem hard to bear
   Under the world's cold scorning,
Sleep softly, friend! new strength will come;
   Kinder will be the morning.

If through the shadows of the night
   Come shapes and sounds of warning,
Bid them avaunt; 'twill all come right,
   God willing, in the morning.

But, O God help thee, friend of mine,
   When sorrow meets thee waking,
And wounds the sunshine cannot cure
   Gape in a heart that's breaking;

When glad "good-morrows" dreamed, are not,
    Must ever be, unspoken;
When morning trills her harp in vain,
    While one sweet wire is broken!

Ah, when that silver cord was loosed,
    Swiftly the parting quiver
Sent waves of harmony, to break
    Over beyond the river.

Remember ever, friend of mine,
    The clang you heard at breaking
Was but a cry just out of sleep,
    Herald of glad awaking.

For you a few more cloudy morns,
    Misty with silent sorrow,
Then, guided by those echoed tones,
    You'll find a glad to-morrow.

THE FRIEND IN SHADOW.

THROUGH golden haze of summer sweet
    Into the wood went happy feet;
The birds sang round me, unafraid,
Where shadows into sunshine strayed.

The lark upon the milk-weed swung,
Rocking it when he loudest sung

Of journeys made to ether blue
On ladders made of silver dew;
The cat-bird, in his sober coat,
Mimicked and stole each liquid note;
The housewife, Jenny, brushed her nest
With dusky feathers from her breast,
Chirping the while a tune to me
To say how happy she should be;
The blue-bird, ending flight and wheel,
Flashed close his wing of azure steel,
Flinging from out his vibrant throat
Quiver and trill and mellow note.

So all the birds made friends, but one.
A sober creature, brown and dun,
Looked at me dumbly from the shade,
But not one word of greeting said,
Nor welcomed me, nor said adieu,
As down the dim green aisles he flew.

* * * *

In sombre night, with drooping head,
My heart as heavy as my tread,
I came to hear what they would say,
These friends who sang the roundelay.
Hist! not one note for good or ill,
No cadence soft, no joyous thrill,
From those who said they loved me well
Before the Shadow 'round me fell.
The cricket's chirp, the night-wind's moan,
Seemed saying softly o'er, "Alone!"

While wearily, with constant drip,
The streamlet wet its rocky lip.

I folded up my hands to say,
"Friendship is only for a day,"
When from the nearest shadow stole
An answer to my troubled soul;
And by the moonbeams scant and pale
I heard the faithful nightingale:
Like silver notes from blue-bells swung,
Like tender tones of human tongue,
Like golden cymbals clanging sweet,
Like castanets on fairies' feet,
Came forth that welcome, strangely dear,
To soothe my sorrow-freighted ear.
Ah, then I knew I had one friend,
Whose love with sunshine did not end.

ONE FOREST-FIRE.

IT'S easy to read it. It's only a word,
Jest a name amongst others—You've heard
Of the fire in the forest?—not much, but you see,
When you read "Simon Podder," that's me.
And it wa'n't no great shakes of a shanty, I know,
But I tell you, I hated to see the thing go;
For one kind o' clings to a ruff he has raised,
And a cabin built out of the trees he has blazed.
But the old house is nothin', I soon let it go;
'Tain't that, that upsets me and worrits me so;

But it's 'bout little Bennie. You heerd of it? Ay,
I can't take it patient, to onct, though I try.

   *   *   *   *

Me and Mary had watched ev'ry evenin' by turn,
Lookin' out fur the wind and the chance of a burn.
Till the smoke settled down to the ground ev'rywhar,
We couldn't see sunset, nor make out a star.
Little Bennie had gathered a heap on the floor—
His new Sunday jacket he never had wore,
His best bow and arrows, his little old spade,—
They were all in a bundle so keerfully laid.
An' Mary had tied up her notions with care;
There was picturs, an' Bibles, an' dead folks' hair,
Huddled in with the spoons Mary's grandmother give
When we bid her good-bye and come out here to
  live.
By'm bye, on the edge of the clearin' in sight,
The smoke it got redder, some sparks seemed to light;
Then the wind fanned it up with a roar like the sea,
Until Mary and Bennie looked fearful at me.
"We must fight it!" I took off the coat that I wore;
Mary picked up her blanket. We turned from the
  door,
Leavin' Bennie a-waitin'. We told him he must,
Till we beat out the fire. Well, he whimpered at
  fust;
But when I looked back he was wipin' his eyes
On his old jacket-sleeve. Then he looked at the
  skies,
And I guessed he was sayin' his Sunday-school prayer,
As he used to o' nights kneelin' down by a chair.

Well, we slapped an' we fought at the fire, with a will,
But the sneakin' red flame in the grass wasn't still,
An' kept creepin' along like a snake. By and by
Mary dropped her burnt shawl with a terrible cry:
Fur there, right between the old shanty and me,
There was winrows of blazes, so we couldn't see
Cabin, chimbley, or haystack or little brown door—
An' we never did see 'em, to speak of, no more.
You've laid little children, maybe, in the dust,
And you thought then the Master had treated you
      wust ;
But you haven't had trouble like Mary an' me ;
You haven't got always a pictur to see
Of a poor little shaver, with tears in his eyes,
Lookin' up kind o' scart to the fire-reddened skies.
That is trouble, I take it, fur Mary an' me—
Worse trouble than ever you're likely to see.

THE WAXEN LILY.

IT came to pass, in the Hexagon
   (The monarchy of the honey-bee),
There arose a murmur of discontent—
   Rebellion against authority.

For Wax, who builded the storehouse walls,
   In his anger spake : "For love or fee
I'll serve no longer these baser needs,
   Building up caskets unceasingly.

THE WAXEN LILY.

"Plummet and measure and crystal square,
    Measure and plummet and spider-line,—
For ever a cell built like the last,
    To treasure the store of amber wine.

"There are better things beneath the sky.
    I saw a maiden with simple skill
From wax carve deftly the petals out
    And the rounded cup of a daffodil!"

Then, by and by, out of heat and pain,
    It found the bliss of a granted prayer,
And awoke one day in the likeness made
    Of a waxen lily gleaming fair—

So fair, that all who above it bent
    Stooped lower to catch its rare perfume,
Then turned away from the smooth deceit
    Of a scentless lily's soulless bloom.

Ah! then it longed for the days of yore,
    Beneath the monarchy's light control,
Shaping honest angles day by day,
    Where none came asking the absent soul.

Weary at last of a life so false,
    It looked for help to the fervid sun,
Who kissed it down into nothingness,
    Glad that the work of its life was done.

TRACKS IN THE SNOW.

TRACKS out over the wide white snow,
  Tracks this morning in rank and row,
Broidered and braided in pearly dun—
Worked with the light of the early sun.

See! on the sides of the lonely road,
Where the woodman goes with a creaking load,
Yon hieroglyphics; look you well,
By the seeded plume of the pimpernel,

How a beaten track, as of little toes,
Hither, and thither, and yonder, goes:
An unthrifty chipmunk, out of food,
Forages now in the winter wood.

Lighter and tinier, here and there,
Like a line engraving, faint and fair,
I see the path where the sparrow trod—
Wee, trustful pensioner of God.

His monogram has the rabbit cut,
With a flying leap and a huddled foot;
Hot-pressed on the snowy page it lies:
"Bunny, his mark"—not over-wise.

Down by the spring, around the stack,
About the barn, up hill and back,
The heavy hoofs of the patient kine
Dug tiny wells in a double line.

Nearer the town, see pussy's mark,
Silently made while it was dark,
Telling of some soft-footed raid
Among the bright-eyed rodents made.

Tracks, as of tardy or busy feet,
Tangle themselves on the village street—
Here a schoolboy's tread, there a woman's shoe,
By a crunching boot-heel cut in two.

Where did they go, those feet gone by?
Whence did they come, and when and why?
Who watched for them, or cared to know
Whose footfall stirred the threshold snow?

Made with a careless tramp they lie,
Telling their tale to you and I,
But cunning hand nor guiding brain
Could fill each snow-white grave again,

And leave it as it laid last night,
Unstirred, and innocent, and white;
Nay, though we sift snow-crystals in,
It will not be what it has been.

We cannot fill the tracks we make;
Our clumsy touch would mar and break;
Only the downfall from above
Can do that wondrous work of love.

LITTLE JO.

WHAT will the birds do, mother, this spring—
    The little brown birds that come to the door?
Will they tap on the window or hop on the step,
    Asking why little Jo wanders out nevermore?

What will the kitten do, mother, alone?
    Will she stop in her frolics a day,
Or lie on the rug by the side of my bed,
    As she did when I once went away?

And Tiger! Oh, mother, love Tiger for me,
    For I know he will mourn for me true;
So keep him when idle and useless he grows,
    Sleeping all the long summer day through;

And show him my coat, so he will not forget
    Little master, who then will be dead;
And speak to him softly and often of "Jo,"
    Stroking slowly his shaggy black head.

And what will old Thomas the gardener say
    When they ask for white blossoms for me?
Will he gather the rose he has tended so long,
    The first fairest bloom on the tree?

I have seen the tears come in his honest old eyes,
    Though he told me the wind brought them there,
As he looked at my cheek growing thinner each day,
    While his hand trembled over my hair.

And dear Uncle Jack, in the far-away camp,
  Will look sad o'er the letter you'll write;
Only say, dearest mother, "Jo's gone to the front,
  Marching nearer and nearer the light."

And you, mother darling—
                You will miss me a while,
  But in heaven no larger I'll grow;
So any kind angel will know when you ask
  At the gate for your own little Jo.

GRANNIE'S TEST.

DEAR grannie is with us no longer;
  Her hair, that was white as the snow,
Was parted one morning for ever
  On her head lying softly and low;
Her hands left the Bible wide open,
  To tell us the road she had trod,
With waymarks like footsteps to tell us
  The path she had gone up to God.

No wonderful learning had grannie,
  She knew not the path of the stars,
Nor aught of the comet's wide cycle,
  Nor Nebula's dim cloudy bars;
But she knew how the wise men, adoring,
  Saw a star in the east long ago;
She knew how the first Christmas anthem
  Came down to the shepherds below.

She never had heard of Hugh Miller,
  Nor knew what philosophers said;
The birthday of each, was a problem
  Which never disturbed her old head.
About the pre-Adamite fossils
  No mental disturbance she knew,
Holding fast to her faith, pure and holy,
  That her God-given Bible was true.

She had her own test, I remember,
  For people, whoe'er they might be.
When we spoke of the strangers about us
  But lately come over the sea—
Of Laura, and Lizzie, and Jamie,
  And stately old Essellby Oakes—
She listened and whispered it softly,
  "My dear, are these friends *meetin'-folks?*"

When our John went away to the city
  With patrons whom all the world knew
To be sober and honest, great merchants,
  For grannie, this all would not do,
Till she pulled at John's sleeve in the twilight,
  To be certain before he had gone;
And he smiled as he heard the old question,
  "Are you sure they are meetin'-folks, John?"

When Minnie came home from the city,
  And left heart and happiness there,
I saw her close kneeling by grannie,
  With the dear wrinkled hands on her hair;

And amid the low sobs of the maiden
    Came softly the tremulous tone,
"He wasn't like meetin'-folks, Minnie;
    Dear child, you are better alone."

And now from the corner we miss her,
    We hear that reminder no more;
But still, unforgotten, the echo
    Comes back from that far-away shore;
Till Sophistry slinks in the corner,
    Tho' Charity sweet has her due,
Yet we feel, if we want to meet grannie,
    'Twere best to be "meetin'-folks," too.

NOBODY KNOWS.

I ASKED the bee in the lily's cup
What held the waxen stamens up,
Or shut each eve its walls of white
About its shaft of malachite;
But the velvet bee, thigh-laden, rose
And grumbled, passing, "Nobody knows."

I asked the crow 'mid the springing corn
How the living blade from the seed was born.
Saucy and sure of his mate's applause,
He answered me prompt and pertly, "Caws;"
But a cricket, hopping between the rows,
Chirped out audibly, "Nobody knows."

I asked the pilot far out at sea
Why the needle turned unfailingly
To the star that gems the northern sky,
But I waited long for his reply,
Till the sounding breakers nearer rose,
And the pilot shouted, "Nobody knows."

I asked the oak how its tent of shade
Without a hammer or saw was made—
How its beams were out on the soft air laid,
And its wide roots sodded without a spade.
A robin sang, "How the oak tree grows,
Nor you, nor I, nor the oak tree, knows."

I asked the moth how the light should be
One light, yet braided with agents three.
The silly thing at my question flew
Around the taper, across, and through,
Scorching and soiling feet and clothes;
Then tracked from an ink-blot, "Nobody knows."

And so I turned to the puzzled saint
Whose faith in the things unseen grew faint,
And bid him wait till he bathed his eyes
In the purer dew of Paradise
Ere he questioned here why life has woes,
When a lily's framing nobody knows.

OLD. SCHOOL AND NEW.

A NGRY and swelling, fierce and fast,
  Ran wide the waves of Schism,
Estranging friends on either bank
  Blessed with a common chrism.
At first it ran a tiny rill
  Between two heads of clover;
At last it ran an angry flood
  Dim eyes could scarce see over.
This side the Old School gravely walked,
  And preached and prayed and pondered;
That side the New School talked and prayed,
  As down the stream it wandered.

From either side the shout went up,
  " Come over, friends, come hither!
The lamp of Life shines on us both
  From yonder surging river."

Each earnest envoy trimmed his bark,
  Each bore the anchor golden,
Forged by Westminster's prayerful ones
  In council grave and olden;
Each to the beacon gladly came
  For better light.
                    Lo! gleaming,
One torch burnt blue upon the waves,
  One ruddy rays sent streaming
Athwart the Doctrine Islands there,
  Jagged and fearful lying,

Scaring the timid sailors back,
  To harbors safer flying.

At last an angel softly came—
  Came with a simple story,
Bidding the pilgrims either side
  Walk upward, facing glory.

Then as they skyward took their way,
  Still seeking wisdom higher,
The river seemed again a rill,
  The banks each side drew nigher,
Till friendly faces looked across,
  And parted hands clasped over
The tiny fountain bubbling up
  Between the heads of clover.

Then hand in hand the pilgrims went
  Up to the Gate of Glory;
Old-School and New told to the King
  At last the self-same story.

THE BAGGAGE-WAGON.

IN from the ferry's pulsing door,
  In by the railroad-gate,
Comes all day long the baggage home,
  Mighty in size and weight.

Trunks with their canvas quite unfurled,
  Boxes in woeful trim,

THE BAGGAGE-WAGON.

With garments dried in country sun
   Tumbled and tossed within.

Under the locks what finery
   Lies travel-stained and worn!—
Limp muslins with the sea-kiss on,
   Flounces on fences torn.

(For how could Kitty stop to think
   Of dress on sea-sand wet,
When Fred was whispering the while
   A vow she don't forget?

Or how could Lily spare her flounce,
   Scrambling in breathless fright,
When Silvertop was coming near
   To woo her, if he might?)

Methinks mamma will open wide
   Her pretty eyes to see
How school-boy Fred has packed his trunk
   With trophies recklessly;

Risking by Bramah Pootra eggs
   The shine of Sunday clothes;
A tortoise in the collar-box,
   Birds' nests on satin bows.

But oh! there's baggage coming home
   In yonder jostled pile,
Packed, outward bound, not long ago,
   With jest and happy smile;

Seeking out now a stricken heart,
  Hands that shall softly move
The folded garments with the touch
  We give to things we love.

  * * *

O solemn garments, needed not!
  O childish treasures, dearer far
For wear of little baby-hands
  Than jewels newly burnished are!

O empty glove and kerchief smooth!
  O idle shoe that treads no more
Life's measure to the tune of Time!
  O treasures dropped on Jordan's shore!

I dream to-day as dreamers must;
  I see dim shadows come,
Claiming their own with smile and tear
  As noisy wheels bring baggage home.

NORTH CONWAY.

I HAVE seen a strain of music,
  I have listened with my eyes
To a silent psalm of sunshine
  Underneath the Conway skies.

Listened? Ay, the wondrous beauty
 Form and color blended, wore,
Seemed a full quartette and chorus,
 Singing grandly evermore

Soft and sweet and brightly varied
 On the Saco's silver thread,
Drowsy with the hum of summer,
 Marked by Ceres' golden tread,
With many a rest and bar of sunshine,
 Grace-notes of the starwort pale,
God decks the calm and clear soprano
 Of Conway's lovely intervale.

Deeper, fuller, stronger, slower,
 Rising, falling, soberly,
Droop the Ledges' rocky billows
 On the tide of harmony:
Holding fast the theme for ever,
 Bidding Echo bide her time;
So the alto of the Ledges
 Bears its part throughout the chime.

There along the near horizon,
 Clear and bare the mighty hills
Send their harmony eternal
 Down to us on summer rills,
Braiding with the silent music—
 Soundless songs that seem to float
Over souls alive with beauty—
 The tenor of the mountain's note.

Listen now, while mighty Nature
    Bares her great vibrating heart,
And calls a measure still and stately,
    Unfettered by the rules of Art;
Who can fail to catch the thunder
    Of the White Hills' solemn base,
With chorded peaks and note triumphant,
    Uplifted to its Maker's face?

Round about the chorus swelling,
    Chicarua and Kearsarge rise,
With Jockey Cap and Peaked Mountain,
    All singing to the Conway skies.
This was the psalm I saw this summer;
    This was the anthem which I heard;
My soul and I alone together
    Without the sound of mortal word.

LADY-BUG.

LADY-BUG lived in a folded rose,
    A petty and dainty aristocrat,
With only a thought for her gaudy clothes,
    Her scarlet cloak and her velvet hat.
Her poor relations, the busy ants,
    She saw go busily travelling past,
And wondered much "why the common herd
    Always hurried so—why they walked so fast;
She never did." In her folded rose
    She moved about with languid grace,

While the morning brought her sun and dew
  To anoint and polish her idle face.
The sunshine lighted her rosy room,
  Perfumed and warm was the air within,
And all the span of the August days
  She needed not either toil or spin.

And so the time of the summer passed,
  While provident ants went hurrying by,
Till tempests threatened the garden-queen,
  And clouds went drifting across the sky.
Lady-bug crept to the rose's heart,
  But found, alas! it was strangely chill;
She ventured out on a strong green leaf,
  But found her world looking damp and ill.

"Along the muddy and tarnished way
  Could she, a Lady-bug, walk? Not she.
She could not plod like the vulgar ants;
  Some other way there would doubtless be."

Still, one by one went the rosy walls,
  Worn by the tempest and soaked with mist,
And the chilling winds whistled round about;
  The sun neglected to keep its tryst;
Louder and stormier grew the blast;
  The scattered leaves flitted far and wide,
Until at last not a petal pale
  Bid the Lady-bug in its shelter bide.

Then she bethought her of sundry ants,
  "Who were all akin, quite a near relation;

Busy sordid souls, but a thrifty folk,
  Filling fairly their humble station.
She had kept aloof from her friends too long;
  She would make amends this morning."
Alas! it was quite too late to learn
  The way she had long been scorning.

*   *   *

All warm and dry with winter store,
  Safe in their castle lying,
The ants knew not that Lady-bug
  Hungry and cold was dying,
Until the storm had passed away,
  And then quite dead they found her,
With all her chilly feet drawn up,
  And faded cloak around her.

SANTA CLAUS'S MISTAKE.

SANTA CLAUS came with a Christmas load
  Over the housetops white;
His reindeer knew all the trodden way
  They had travelled each Christmas night.
The old saint gurgled a cheery laugh
  As he stopped by the chimney-top;
His very cap was agog with fun
  When the bright stars saw him drop.

He shook himself from the cloud of soot,
  Then looked on a little chair;

He looked on the bed so smooth and white;
. On the shelf, but it was not there;
Under the mantel's shadowy side;
   Up on the pantry-door;
But the little stocking he could not find
   He had always found before.

He softly gathered again his gifts;
   His face was a sight to see
As tears fell down on his furry coat,
   And he said, "No work for me;
I'm only a jolly childish saint;
   I cry, but can do no more;
Only the Christ-child's tender feet
   Should come to the silent door."

He stole away, but the reindeers' bells
   He stuffed with the woolly snow,
So the stricken mother could hear him not
   As he softly went, and slow.

     *   *   *   *

A timid knock at the barrèd door;
   A rush of the midnight air;
A pleading voice, and before them stood,
   As they opened, the Christ-child fair.

"I come," he said, "to the lonely arms
   That are vacant except for me;
Oh take me in; I have walked to you
   From the shores of Galilee.

I saw as I passed by the angels' road
  Where the feet of your child had been;
I saw the shine of the crystal bars
  As they lowered to let him in."

  * * * *

So the Christ-child came in the holy night,
  And tarried the darkness through;
But was gone at morning,—how or when
  None watching or waiting knew;
But evermore through the Christmas chime
  For a knock will the lone hearts wait,
While Santa Claus, with his muffled bells,
  Goes sorrowing past the gate.

THE FAIRIE FERN.

I LISTENED to Flite in his gilded cage—
Listened and nodded above my page—
Listened and nodded; and then—and then—
I was far away from the haunts of men,
Where a virgin forest about me stood
Columned and leafy, a summer wood,
Filled with the quiver of rushing wings
And songs of the feathered and happy things.

Softly the Queen of the Fairies laid
On my ear a fern—'twas an accolade,
And I rose her knight, true and loyal fay,
Who knew what the birds say day by day.

'Twas a wondrous world which I entered then;
I shall never tell where it lies, to men,
For the Fairie Queen, ere she left me, said
Revengeful pinions would beat me dead
If I their haunts to the world betrayed,
Or a gun should enter the sylvan shade;
But all they whistled, or said, or sung
I might translate into human tongue.

A kindred city it seemed to ours,
For all its dwellings were leafy bowers,
For all its bipeds were minus boots,
Guiltless of trains or Sunday suits;
For all they build in the selfsame way
As the birds who sang in the world's first May;
For all this, strangely familiar seemed
The wild birds' chatter of which I dreamed.

Flitting in haste through the leafy street,
I heard them talk about "Bills to meet;"
Of the new "air-line that was up to par,"
And the debt which came through the "Magpie
    war;"
Of the "Brook-line bridge," which they did not
    need;
Of the fearful price of canary-seed;
Who should be envoy, and what the terms
For the great "New Diet"—that of Worms.

Sounds as of Babel filled the glen
(In Bird-land banks all close at ten):

"What are the bids for Eyrie stock?"
"What is the time by Clytie's clock?"
"What does the Carrier-Pigeon bring?"
"Columbia's eagle has hurt her wing;"
"Poor Lark is dead! left a helpless wife!"
"Insured? Oh yes! in the 'New York Life;'"
"So she will have only grief to bear,
Without the pressure of daily care."
"What tidings under the Seabird's wing?"
"A ship aground, like an idle thing;
Her cargo lost! her crew afloat
On the open sea in a leaky boat."
"Where's Corvus gone? Ah! don't you know
He was a most dishonest crow?
A corporation in black coats
Levied on grain-fields, paid in notes
Uncurrent, and all fled but he,
Who swings on yonder apple tree."

The while this noisy chat goes on,
The Lady-birds have been since dawn
Singing, to stretch their little throats,
Brushing their glossy redingotes,
Daintily lining rounded nests,
Carefully brushing snowy vests,
Chattering, oh, so loud and clear,
I held my breath their tones to hear.

"Old Rusty Rook a book has written;"
"Ann Oriole gave Jay the mitten;"

"Miss Nightingale can't sing at all;"
"Bob Lincoln gave a hop last fall;"
"The charming tenor have you heard?
A most accomplished foreign bird."
(The while two mother Robins fought
About their broods as no birds ought.)

Oh touch me with thy fairie fern;
No language new, O Queen, I'll learn;
'Tis the same story o'er and o'er;
Arcadia's gone—it comes no more.

I wake and nod before the fire,
While Flite sings through his golden wire.

COURAGEOUS FEAR.

THERE was war and disorder;
　　The bulbs in the border
Had mutinied, led by the sun;
　　Mother Earth, their adviser,
　　Had told them 'twas wiser
To wait 'till the frost's work was done.

　　Very softly and slowly,
　　With love true and holy,
She laid her brown hands on each head
　　In the old mother fashion,
　　Full of tender compassion,
In spite of the brave words they said.

With trust of the fearless,
With joy of the tearless,
With faith by the traitor untried,
    They clamored and crowded,
    And slowly unshrouded,
To fight for the guerdon denied:

    "Shall we be belated?
    The birds have all mated,
For Robin the tale told to-day;
    Gay sunshine is calling,
    The tender dew falling;
Then why should a flower-bulb stay?

    "Mother Earth can't compel us
    To stay, though she tell us
Of north wind, and ice on the lawn;
    She has grown grim and older,
    Her feelings are colder,
Her youthful vivacity gone."

    They were up in the border,
    The gay ranks in order,
When, lo! came the Northman, Jack Frost;
    He chanced to remember
    A sunny December,
So made up the time he had lost.

    Then the corps so defying
    Fell blasted and dying,
All struck by the terrible spear;

Making humble confession
And late-learned concession,
That Earth had been wise in her fear.

GOLD AND CRIMSON.

O SWEET September idleness!
  O castle-wall in Spain!
O leaves of gold and crimson,
  Wet with November rain!
How many days have come and gone
  Since you, and I, and Fate,
Despatched two tiny ventures out
  With only Hope for freight?

Two maple leaves—one forest-gold,
  And one the sunset red—
We flung upon the valley-stream,
  And watched them as they sped.
Close to the shore they fluttered down,
  Each pretty Dryad boat,
Made mystical by rite and spell—
  Your life and mine afloat.

Amid the shadows for a while
  They glided still and slow,
Until a current's rippled edge
  Caught them and bid them go.
The golden craft stole silently
  Around the island shore,

While underneath the rustic bridge,
  The red, her colors bore.

A willow weeping by the bank
  Swept in the ruddy spark,
That shone amid her sombre shade
  Like firelight through the dark.
Swiftly the golden shallop sped,
  Its destiny the sea,
Till, rescued by a zephyr's breath,
  The red joined company.

Then came the gust of angry wind
  That parted gold and red,
And left the riddle of our lives
  For evermore unread.
Hast thou, O friend, the harbor made?
  Say, was thy journey long?
Were rocks and currents merciful?
  Did Sirens cheat with song?

Shall we each other meet again
  Where ocean tides begin,
And life-boats launched in sombre shade,
  Through sunshine enter in?
I may not know, yet in my dreams
  That fairy race I see,
When crimson, grounded by the wood,
  And gold, went to the sea.

THE SUNKEN ISLAND.

O'ER Canaderaga the shadows creep,—
　Dreams of her silent summer sleep;
Yon pictured hill, a blue-veined lid,
Curtains the brightness beneath it hid;
The toying tress of the willow swings,
And the tasselled birch her guerdon flings,
Till the wave wakes up from its revery,
And, Indian-like, laughs silently.

In shore, the tall flags moveless stand,
With lances straight like warder band,
To guard the lily's jewelled cup,
Whose golden wine the wave bears up;
But guards in vain: the robber bee
Drinks and away, humming merrily,
And the dragon-fly waves its wing of light
Into the sunshine and out of sight.

But just where the mountain-shadows break
Lies the sunken isle of the laughing lake,
Where the soft green rushes idly sway,
And the fisher's boat is seen alway,
As the angler peers through the limpid wave
For a glimpse of the island's lonely grave,
And dreams of the time when in air it stood,
With its crown of flowers and belt of wood.

For Canaderaga a legend keeps,
To be whispered low when the midnight creeps

THE SUNKEN ISLAND.

Moonless and still on the lonely shore—
A tale of the lost for evermore.

Far back in the land of the Long Ago
Stood an island fair in the summer glow,
Where ever alone a prophet dwelt,
For whose healing touch the suffering knelt.
Thither the Mohawk warrior came
With the wound from poison-dart aflame;
And the Iroquois, with his war-won pain,
Sought at his hand for health again.

Savage of mien and dark of mood,
As well became his Indian blood,
Sullen and stern, none ever guessed
The secrets locked in the dusky breast;
Knew not how oft in the swift canoe
The shivered waves from the paddles flew,
As close by the dim deep forest stayed
The prophet's foot in the darkness strayed,
Till close by the bitter fountain's brink
He stopped at last, yet not to drink ;
But bore from thence the wondrous draught,
The source and secret of his craft.

At last, the olden legend saith,
He claimed the power to conquer Death ;
And spoke in horrid blasphemy
Of twinship with Divinity;
Then the Great Spirit's awful frown
Sent isle and prophet hurtling down ;

And wondering pilgrims to that shore
Saw isle or prophet nevermore.

The sunken island! Ah, 'twere well
If only legends wild could tell
The tale. On Life's broad sea
Such things as these there often be—
Bright spots that softly shine and gleam,
Fair as a sinless angel's dream—
And yet they sink, and all but we
Go floating on right merrily.

So each alone his secret keeps,
Where his lost vision bides and sleeps—
Sails bravely on, and makes no moan
Over the fairy landscape gone;
Yet glancing where the rushes grow,
Bent by the breath of the Long Ago,
He says no word, but dreams the while
Of the unforgotten Sunken Isle.

"RACK-O'-BONES."

PULL with a will at the work-house bell!
The beggar sleeps in his coffin well—
Ring with an echo; he won't awake!
Such sleep, such music, will never break.

Fold up his hands on his pauper shroud,
He has fallen back from the busy crowd—
Back from the haunts that have known him stepped—
Back to a merciful Maker crept.

Somebody tenderly smooth his hair
On his forehead cold; it once was fair.
A mother loved him—somebody say
A pitiful word; a blossom lay
On his breast—not rare ones born in bowers,
But sun-bright daisies, wayside flowers,
Such as God gives to the beggar's hand,
As thick as their silver crowns can stand.

Somebody think what his life has been—
Solemn with sorrow and soiled with sin;
Goaded by treason, by hunger tried;
Longing for good, yet unsatisfied;
Nameless, except for a pauper jest
Whose title touches his slenderness.
Hither at last has the pathway led—
From a cradle down to a work-house bed.

Somebody think! Did he ever pray,
Or ever know how the beggar lay
On the good man's breast in Paradise,
Whom Dives saw with his longing eyes?
Did no one read to him that great will
Which made him rich, though a beggar still?
Did no one tell him about the Friend
Who over the lowliest one will bend?

"Ay! under his folded suit of gray
A well-worn Bible was found, they say."
Ring loudly, bells! quiver loud and clear!
No beggar lies in the coffin here;
There's one plate less, there's an empty chair—
One patient less for the matron's care;
The night is stiller without his moans.
Ring! daylight's come to "Rack-o'-bones."

DON'T WAKE THE BABY.

FORGET the parcel you should bring
    From town; forget the bonnet
With dainty plume and twisted bow,
    And—little bill pinned on it;
Tell Madame Basque to trim with folds,
    Instead of fringe and laces,
The pretty dress your wife will wear
    In triumph at the races.

Put up your boots on brocatel,
    Smoke parlor-curtains yellow;
'Twill only bring a mild reproof,
    Like this: "You bearish fellow,
I never saw such careless ways;
    No, Fitz Adolphus, never!"
But then a kiss or coaxing word
    Will right the wrong for ever.

Bring home a friend with you to dine
    When cook is out, or going;
Leave little knots of ribbon blue
    Upon your dress-coat showing;
Forget the date of wedding-day;
    Pronounce her pastor fusty;
Insinuate her poodle dog
    Is neither kind nor trusty.

For these you *may* atonement make,
    And hope to be forgiven
(There might be trouble, I admit,
    About the knot of ribbon;
But with a show of penitence
    And compliments judicious,
You might convince your wife at last
    You were not truly vicious).

But don't you wake the baby, friend,
    With creaking boot advancing;
Step on your tiptoes as you go,
    Like bear or monkey dancing;
For if you wake that baby, friend,
    That mother, sternly rising,
Will then and there bestow rebuke
    With energy surprising.

Ah, kisses then will be in vain,
    In vain your speeches tender,
And baby will tear up the rose
    Your penitence may send her.

So, if you would be truly wise,
   And risk a lecture never,
Don't wake the baby sleeper, friend,
   And be beloved for ever.

BRIDGES.

BY the still meadow-stream,
   Where the childish feet strayed,
Two eyes, bright and wistful,
   Looked downward afraid
At the sodden green rushes,
   The soft rippling flow
As it wrinkled the face
   In the water below;
Across at the cowslips
   That, golden and gay,
Nodded softly defiance,
   Then coaxed in their way,
Till a pair of strong arms
   Laid a plank on the clover,
And glad little feet
   Took the eager hands over.

That was long time agone.
   Bridges many I know,
With their second selves painted
   In waters below,

From the chance-levelled bough
　In the shadowy wood,
To the wonderful span
　O'er the down-rushing flood;
But for ever a pathos
　And beauty enshrine
Every bar with its shadow
　Across the wave's shine.
All tell the same tale,
　From the wind-fallen larch
Where the squirrels go free,
　To the ponderous arch;
For there's always in life
　Rapid streams to divide,
And the cowslips *will* grow
　On the opposite side;
So a bridge is a type
　Of our longings confessed,
Out of Life's discontent
　Reaching still for our rest.

We build them of silver,
　With railings of gold,
But the wind of adversity
　Loosens their hold.
We build them of Love,
　And the cable untwists
That was bound round a promise,
　And tied with a kiss.
We build them of Honor;
　Lo! Slander's foul breath

Paints them ruddy with rust
  Till a footfall is death.
We build them of glory;
  The quicksand, ashift,
Leaves the arches all sprung
  And the timbers adrift.

But, thanks be for ever!
  One bridge is all ready;
It lies on the promises,
  Anchored and steady:
'Tis the bridge of the Cross,
  All ashine in the gloom,
And the Lilies of Peace
  On its farther side bloom.

THE GARDEN-GATE.

LONG ago, in childish terror,
  From a fancied gnome I fled,
Casting frightened glances backward,
  Longing looks toward home ahead;
Through the lane and by the willows,
  Swift and sure as feet of fate,
Never stayed I till behind me
  Clanged and clasped the garden-gate.

Blessed gate of happy childhood,
  Barring harm and sorrow out,

Where the shadow of the homestead
  Threw protection round about!
Blessed warders, peace and safety,
  Holding watch for wanderer late,
Closing with their arms about me
  When I shut the garden-gate!

All things fearsome lay before it,
  Springing foe and lurking wile;
All things true and right within it
  Clustered round my mother's smile;
But the years came creeping, creeping—
  Years that would not bide and wait—
Till, despite my bitter weeping,
  Foes came through the little gate.

Haggard Care, with restless finger,
  Clutched and rattled at the latch,
Time, with silent saw and hammer,
  Hacked full many a ragged scratch;
Lean Distrust came through the crevice;
  Disappointment leaped across;
And ruddy War, with lurid lightning,
  Marked thereon the bloody cross.

Ah, how I struggled when the stranger,
  Pale and terrible and grim,
Unclasped the hands that fain would hold it
  As he came through twilight dim.
"A little while, O pallid Stranger!
  A year!—a day!—a moment wait!

We love him so!" Death gave no answer,
   Except to come within the gate.

And now I know that safe no longer
   Falls the cottage-latch for me,
Though I waiting watch beside it
   With weary head and bending knee;
Yet with eyelids closed and weary,
   Quite forgetting day or date,
I dream again how bright the heaven
   Whose portal was the garden-gate.

THE WIFE'S LETTER.

"MY letters?" A shapely hand stretched out;
   The gold of a yellow beard was stirred
A moment over the sombre mouth,
   Guiltless of idle or wasted word.

The grasp that had known a sword-hilt well
   Closed tightly over the silent things
Which the postal eddy drifts in heaps
   Where human life to an anchor clings.

This one, with a great official seal,
   And that, with the solemn legal air,
Are opened slowly and gravely read,
   Then closed with a sober, quiet care.

THE WIFE'S LETTER.

"And this!" On the brown face comes a shade;
    The eyes grow dimmer, and strangely dark;
Across the temple there reddens fast
    The line of the rugged sabre-mark.

The solemn glance of the lifted face
    Is over days that have fled for aye;
A comrade sleeps after battle well
    Where the folded tents of the soldiers lie.

A vision comes of a toilsome march,
    A picture made out of battle-smoke—
A reeling form and a crimson pool
    Where the line of battle wav'ring broke.

But this, the name in violet ink,
    The monogram with its letters three!
Above the mouth, see! the hand is laid,
    Lest we, the smile which it hides, may see.

Ah! useless quite is the studied calm;
    Any idler near, the tale may tell
That a thousand miles away, there bides
    A woman fair, and she loves him well.

A gentle light in the eyes that read,
    A smile through the beard and hand betrayed,
A tender care for its folding up
    Before its weight o'er a heart is laid.

Away from common and business words,
    It softly lies like a sacred thing—

An amulet by a fairy blest,
A drifted plume from an angel's wing.

TELL ME, MOTHER.

"TELL me over, mother dear,
How Benny looked when he was here;
I might not know, and pass him by,
Looking along the purple sky.

"Among the harps with golden strings,
Behind the angels' great white wings,
Beside the Lamb or by the gate,
Think you that little Ben will wait?

"I never saw him, don't you know?
He lived and died so long ago,
Before I came. How old was he?
And is he waiting there for me?"

"Tell, you, my darling? If I may
For tears that, choking, fight their way—
Tears for the angel safe at rest,
Tears for the angel on my breast.

"Fragile and white, with mournful eyes,
A tender mouth and brow too wise;
Soft rippling wealth of cloudy gold,
In curl and wavelet, softly rolled

"Over the patient bended back,
Twisted by pain that shamed the rack:
This was our Benny. He was seven
When Jesus took him home to heaven."

"But, mother, will God keep him so?
If not, how ever will I know
His angel there? Oh, hold me tight;
I'm going, mother, home to-night.

"I'll find dear Benny somewhere there;
I'll know the shining of his hair;
And shall I give him your dear love,
To keep till you shall come above?

"I hear sweet music. Mother, see!
A childish presence beckons me;
And oh, where once was twist, and mar,
The shining wings of angels are."

THE LESSON OF A SHADOW.

OLD Uncle Ralph by the cottage sat,
Wearing well-brushed coat, and his Sunday hat,
On the little porch where the shadow sweet
Of the maple boughs, fell across the street.

Lakes of the sunshine, shores of shade,
Islands, and capes, by the light winds made,

Were mapped in gold on the dewy ground,
With a grassy rim like a ribbon round.

And Max, wise Max, in the doorway stood,
In a doubting man's misanthropic mood,
Saying, "Uncle Ralph, may be that is so,
For you, but for me— Unless I know
Through my senses keen—either hear, or see,
Why, the thing itself is unproved to me."

This the phrase I caught out of long debate
On the need of faith in our mortal state,
As I looked the loops of the woodbine through
At the old brown face full of glory new.

"Look yonder, Max." In a pool of sun
Flitted here and hither a shadow dun
Of a little bird that we could not see.
"Can you prove that robin a fact to me?
Do you see the bird? Do you hear it?" "Nay."
"Then there is no bird. Is it thus you say,
Friend Max?" Why, where has the wise man gone,
Leaving Uncle Ralph on the porch alone
To shake his head, while a tender smile
Comes over his patient face the while?

"Only shadows now, but the substance then,"
He said, as the bird trilled a loud "Amen."

SHADOWS OF THREESCORE AND TEN.

DO you remember it, old friend,
   How in the sunny weather
Our morning shadows as we went
   Blended across the heather?

A jagged outline gay and grim,
   Athwart the meadow lying;
With slouching hat now topped, and now
   With curl and veil outflying.

It seemed to wear a blowy beard;
   It seemed to wear long tresses;
There was the flutter of a coat,
   The wave of summer dresses.

Then afterward the sun rose high,
   And though we walked together
Along the road, two shadows blent
   Close round us on the heather.

Only an outstretched hand at last
   Across the sunshine builded
A phantom guide-post, now and then
   With frets of sunlight gilded.

E'en that was slowly washed ashore
   By noontide's flood of glory;
Contentment brought forgetfulness:
   'Tis Life's old common story.

But now, old friend, all journeying
    For us will soon be over;
Sorrow has built a sombre bridge
    With piers of churchyard clover,

Till, blended as they used to be,
    Our shadows, longer growing,
Lie yonder on the other side,
    Over the white snow showing

A bended head, a planted staff,
    Nor trees nor kerchief blowing;
The Shadow lies behind us, friend—
    The light, the way we're going.

EARTH'S ANGELS.

I NEVER knew an angel,
    Except the ones in books;
I don't believe a mortal
    Knows how an angel looks.
We guess at something misty
    With trailing wings of white,
With amber tresses floating,
    And garments strangely bright.

But I believe earth's angels
    Walk here in mortal guise,
Though we discern but faintly
    Through heavy-lidded eyes,

Or see them as they leave us
    Who walk beside us here,
Their angelhood quite hidden,
    Because it lives so near.

I can remember angels
    Who seemed like common folks,
Who wore old-fashioned bonnets
    And faded winter cloaks;
Who came when dire disaster
    Crowned lesser home mishap,
Or younger claimants crowded
    The dear maternal lap—

With curving arms wide open
    To take the weary in,
With patient love to listen
    To childish want or sin.
What better thing could angels
    For childish sinners do
Than listen to their story
    And bid them promise new?

I think of fireside angels,
    Upon whose faded hair
There shone no crown of glory,
    And yet the crown was there,
When tender love, true-hearted,
    Forgave the wrongs it knew,
And patient voice gave answer
    The days of trial through.

Ah me! the childish angel
  Who beckons as I write!
Perchance I should not know him
  In mystic robe of white;
He wears a school-boy's jacket,
  And cap and boots to me,
As when we talked at twilight,
  His head against my knee.

There are dear mother-angels—
  We each perchance know one—
Whose robes of better glory
  Are daily being spun—
With loving hands to guide us,
  With loving speech to cheer.
Said I not well, earth-angels
  Walk daily with us here!

THE SHIP OF THE SUMMER-TIME.

O FAIR, blooming summer! I watch for you still;
I wait till the hours shall your cloud-shallop fill,
And, freighted with flowers and singing-birds sweet,
You float over coming days close to my feet.

New leaves in the forest, new buds on the bough,
New grain foaming up from the track of the plough;
New blooms in the garden, new nests in the tree;—
Ah! everything's new every summer but me.

Ay, even the sand, that was level before,
Now drifts in a mound on the time-beaten shore;
A rift in the heart and a sigh in the breast
Since a twelvemonth ago are as new as the rest.

One more breezy May, one glowing June more,
Come in as I watch on the rocks by the shore,
Where broken ships lie with the sea-weed about,
And the little waves laugh at the kelson so stout,

Singing soft all the day, merry songs in the sun,
As over the wrecks, with their white feet they run—
The wrecks of the years, fast aground from the tide,
All sodden and black on the wild ocean-side.

O ship of the summer! what bring you to me?
What chances and changes with blossoming tree?
What light glaring glows in the faint August noon?
What dark shadows wait for the soft harvest moon?

What sorrowful budget is hid in your hold?
What sigh lies asleep in your sail's snowy fold?
What heart will you cleave with your incoming
        prow?
O ship of the summer-time! whisper it now,—

So that ere thou comest so swiftly to me,
I may fashion a pennon of quaint broiderie,
With this for its motto: "Whatever betide,
I'll follow the Master, I'll trust in my Guide."

And if I come then to the May-buds no more,
But sleep with the leaves on the October shore,
I'll fold up my hands as I cling to the mast,
Looking up to the flag till the earth-lights are passed.

THE GRAY BOATMAN.

"WHITHER, oh whither, boatman,
    With your garb of hodden gray?
From whence, and what your errand?
    And where will you land, I pray?"

"I come with the king's commission,
    Still seeking if I may find
On shore, in the hall, or hamlet,
    One ever-contented mind.

"I come from the mountain-streamlet;
    I've carried my gray canoe
Around where the rocks are roughest;
    The rapids I've battled through.

"I've been at the woodman's cottage,
    I've answered the castle's call;
But the jewel that tests the question
    Grows paler before them all."

Then I saw on his broad breast lying
    An opal without its spark,

Like a crystal lamp unlighted,
    A home with its hearthstone dark.

"I've sailed on the silent river,
    Still tacking from shore to shore,
But the soulless opal never
    A flash for a claimant bore.

"My lord from the castle yonder
    Quite failed with the magic spell,
For he envied a shooting-manor
    A neighbor would never sell.

"My lady, with jewels shining,
    Called not from the gem a ray,
For the bitter sigh of the childless
    Was biding beneath alway.

"The painter with nodding laurel,
    The poet with fadeless bay,
Courtier, and hind, and maiden,
    Each bade me a moment stay;

"But the poet would be a Milton,
    The painter-lad loved in vain,
And the courtier's foot was gouty;
    So I seaward turn again.

"Far down in the quiet valley
    I'll tarry at eventide,

  Where the stones of the marble village
   Stand thickly side by side."

   * * * *

Where a rift in the budding clover
 Had furrowed a rugged mark,
O'er the breast of the silent sleeper
 To the opal came back its spark.

THE OLD DOORSTONE.

"I AM going, old house! You belong to a stranger,
 Old house, that was Eden in days that are o'er.
I am going, old garden! Good-bye!" How I linger
 Upon the stone step that is close by the door!—

Worn by the footsteps of those who have loved me;
 Worn by the tread that shall pass it no more;
Worn by the feet that walked in at the threshold,
 But outward were borne through the wide-open door;

Rosy with flowers we twined in the spring-time,
 Blushing with blossoms the summer-time bore,
Littered with golden-hued leaves of the autumn,
 Or mantled in snow, lay the stone by the door.

There, sit at eventide, memories tender,
 And shadows of day-dreams that died long ago;
These, sweeter than roses and fairer than flowers—
 Those, sadder than autumn leaves, colder than snow.

THE OLD DOORSTONE.

Come hither, sweet visions, crouch low by the lintel;
  Look up in my face with the love-light of yore,
And bid me forget how fast years have flitted
  Since I saw you at sunset around the old door.

Brave Arthur and Robbie, with boyhood's clear glances,
  Come back from your homes by the far ocean-shore;
And golden-haired sister, creep lovingly hither;
  We used to sit thus on the step by the door.

Dear mother, with smile like the face of an angel;
  And father beloved— Ah, memory sore!
Low-drooping, the wing of the Death-Angel rustled,
  And swept as it passed, o'er the step by the door.

You remember, old stone, how twilight one summer,
  The twilight and I, heard vows whispered o'er?
Never mind it, old stone; I live and am patient,
  Tho' I sit all alone on the step by the door.

And great shaggy Bruno, true, honest and loving—
  Old Bruno has gone from the spot in the sun;
His eyes, lookingly dumbly such patient devotion,
  Are sleeping for aye; Bruno's night-watch is done.

Good-bye, then, old house; I shall pass you a stranger,
  By fireside or garden to come nevermore;
But I'll glance at the stone, and I'll people its quiet
  With forms that I loved when we sat by the door.

THE SUNSHINE'S STORY.

FOUR little pictures; that was all
    To tell his ended life
To me, a lonely woman still,
    Who should have been his wife.

Out of his mother's feeble hand
    I took them one by one,
To read his story, short and sad,
    Told by the faithful sun.

"This one"—she rubbed it with her sleeve—
    "My eyes can scarcely see;
'Twas taken when he was a boy,
    A dear good boy to me!"

A round and rosy little face,
    With awkward, frightened stare,
And sturdy, nervous school-boy hand
    Clutched tightly on a chair.

"And this was in his college days,
    When he went courting you."
I pulled my veil across my face,
    And near the picture drew.

I saw the eager hazel eyes,
    The careless, wind-tossed hair,
The very knotting of the tie
    I loved to see him wear

When browner shone these locks of mine
    That folded glimmer gray,
When life no dim December knew,
    Only the merry May.

I laid it, with a solemn sigh,
    Softly upon her knee,
Rememb'ring how my stubborn pride
    Had parted him from me—

How bitter pain had followed fast,
    Repentance all too late—
For him, in time, a loveless wife;
    For me, a lonely fate.

'And this," she said, "was best of all,
    But part of it is gone;
I rubbed *her* figure off the plate—
    I could not keep it on."

A bearded mouth, a sterner face
    Than used to smile on me,
A stalwart figure full of grace;
    Beside this I could see

The outline of a woman's dress
    Along the mimic floor;
A blot, large as a woman's hand,
    The shoulder plainly bore.

O blotch, that came so near his heart!
    What pen could better tell

The tale of faithless queen uncrowned!
What picture half so well!

"And this, was taken at Fair Oaks,
    They say.   It came to me
With gun, and cap, and hasty line
    Scrawled lying on his knee."

Over the soldier's solemn face,
    That time shall touch no more,
Nor sunshine find to add a line,
    Nor shadow darken more,

I looked, so I might not forget,
    Then whispered low a prayer,
If I might unto glory come,
    That I should know him there.

A DAY'S CAMPAIGN.

AND so the "campaign of a day" is ended;
    The "house-mother" blesses each sleepy head,
And for flag of truce, holds out a pillow
    Before the camp of the children's bed.

Now she counts the cost of the day just ended
    By the tingling nerves at her finger-tips,
And seals the last of her war-despatches
    On the childish brows with her loving lips.

There was "muster" first in the early morning;
  Thank God, that they all might answer "Here!"
There were troops to fit for the hill of Science,
  With many a halt and many a tear.

There were hands and hearts in a skirmish wounded,
  Waiting the touch of her tender hand;
Small uniforms out at knees and elbows,
  And for rations, always a new demand.

There were "shamrock troops" to be safely guided
  Out of the bogs into beaten ways,
And the "needle-corps" to be armed and ready
  For a new advance against coming days.

"Guerilla Care" always hid in ambush
  To catch her sleeve on his thorny spear;
While within herself some traitor weakness
  Whispered at times of failure drear.

Where is the chaplet fit to crown her,
  Thus as she halts when day is done,
With a day's campaign so wisely guided
  Betwixt the dawn and the setting sun?

AT LAST.

"TRAIN from the West!" The parted crowd
  Fell back each side the iron road;
A little hush a moment fell
  Just as the engine screamed and slowed.

Then human atoms outward spilled
   On branching walks and vagrant ways—
Some by Love's waiting magnets drawn
   Out from the shifting, tangled maze;

Some, all unclaimed by love or law,
   Went drifting slowly here and there,
To find within some hostelrie
   The semblance of Love's home and care.

There, till the last faint echo fell,
   An old man waited, worn and gray,
Watching the faces as they passed,
   In hungry, searching, wistful way.

The trackmen tell of vigil kept
   Through counted days of many years—
Waiting at morning, noon and night,
   Untouched by unbelieving sneers—

Waiting, with faith most woman-like,
   The boy who left him long ago—
Waiting the trains as one by one
   From West to East each day they go.

The wand'rer sought the Golden Gate
   Beyond it—where he went, who knows;
They whisper softly, "He has gone,
   Out through the gate that don't unclose."

And yet the old man keeps his faith:
   "My boy is living, well I know;

And he'll come back." Then watches still,
    Through harvest-time, through frost and snow.

"Train from the West!" The father's face
    Is full of hope as still he peers
Along the line of flitting forms,
    As he has done so many years.

No woman's beauty wins his glance,
    Fair tho' it be and smiling sweet;
No white-haired man, or little child,
    Looks up his eager glance to meet.

But bearded faces young and brown,
    He scans each one. The crowd has passed,
And still the old man keeps his place
    To see the laggard who is last.

There is a catch of in-drawn breath,
    An old face eager, white, and wild,
As nearer comes the traveller,
    Until they meet—father and child!

A sturdy shoulder holds the head
    All silver white. The lips are dumb
At first; then trembling fall the words,
    "My lad at last! I knew you'd come!"

No dreamer's story made of mist
    I've threaded into beads of rhyme;
The tale is true as tryst of star,
    Or, promised grain of summer-time.

THE ONES WHO ARE LEFT BEHIND.

AT either end of that sad link
   'Twixt Here, and There, we call Good-bye;
Hands tremble, and the full heart throbs
   For what beyond its length shall lie.

But ah! the trav'ller outward bound
   On yonder sky sees novel gleams,
While waiting ones whose feet are stayed
   Have only memory and dreams.

The bird that leaves its woodland nest
   Catches new sunshine on its wing;
The lonely one that stays at home,
   Brooding in shade, forgets to sing.

The gathered rose by beauty worn
   Flaunts gayly, tho' it dies so soon;
The rifled bush in sorrow bides
   Through starlight watch and sleepy noon.

The country boy with honest heart
   Cityward turns and fights his way;
Pity the lad, but pity more
   The "old folks" who at home must stay.

Bravely the bride at parting turns
   From loving arms about her twined;
Sunlight is o'er thee, bonny bride—
   Shade for the mother left behind.

THE ONES WHO ARE LEFT BEHIND.

So when a good ship sails away,
   I seem to hear upon the wind
Prayers—not for travellers on their way,
   But for the sad hearts left behind,

For whom life has the same routine,
   Only unlighted, as of yore,
By forms and voices loved, and lost
   From stair and hall and open door.

For evermore the strongest go,
   Venturing far—we weak ones stay;
Ora pro nobis, kindly souls,
   As well as those who go away;

And oh, when angels stoop to take
   Buds never lent to blossom here—
When stalwart souls up higher rise,
   For better work in light more clear—

When for the last time lies the link
   'Twixt hands "Good-bye" no more shall bind,
Then, dear Lord, look in mercy down;
   Comfort the sad ones left behind.

THE REASON WHY.

(In answer to the song, "Won't you tell me why, Robin?")

YOU bid me tell you why, Jenny,
    I come no longer near;
You think my heart is cold, Jenny,
    Biding in silence here;
You think I never try the gate
    Nor give you blossoms gay;
I cannot tell you why, Jenny,
    But sighing turn away.

You do not know that late at night
    I kiss the little gate,
Because your hand has rested there
    Its warm and willing weight;
You know not how I treasure up
    The hawthorn spray all torn,
Or that upon my breast there lies
    A blue knot you have worn.

Well, by and by perchance I'll tell,
    And maybe not for ever;
If brother Allan wins you, dear,
    I'll tell the reason—never.
I promised one, an angel now,
    To have him in my keeping—
To guard his golden head from harm,
    His heart from care and weeping.

He whispered in his dream "Jenny,"
  And waking shunned my eye;
And so I gave the lad his chance,
  Though yielding I should die.
So if you love him best, Jenny,
  Although my heart may break,
I'll keep my oath and help the lad,
  For our dead mother's sake;.

And over yonder stormy sea
  I'll take my load of sorrow,
To bear it as I may, till time
  Shall bring some calm to-morrow.
But when I die, above my breast
  The hawthorn tree shall wave—
A knot of ribbon bright and blue
  Rest with me in the grave.

A fortnight more ere I can speak—
  Till then I dare not meet you;
I dare not walk beside you, dear,
  In dance or revel greet you.
Then, if poor Allan bids me ask
  The boon he could not buy,
I'll tell you in the lane, Jenny,
  Softly, "the reason why."

"WITH CARE."

THE sculptor's thought to marble grown,
    Perfect as shapely thought might be,
Laid swathed in wrappings folded close,
    "With care," to cross the land and sea.

Warm with the fair Italian sun,
    They laid the dim white dream away;
Around it pressed the golden straw
    That nodded, growing, yesterday.

The while, some seeds of Southern blooms,
    By no one picked with tender hands—
(At least no man; the Lord of all
    Its passport gave to foreign lands),

Were nestled there in Tuscan straw,
    Each robing folded from the air;
So germs as well as marble went
    Beneath the painted mark, "With care."

Safe to the far-off Northern port,
    Safe to the waiting Northern town,
True hands the statue safely bore,
    And all unblemished laid it down.

Safely they reared the wondrous shaft
    Amid the palace columns' gleam,
And men became idolaters
    Before Thorwaldsen's "frozen dream."

Meanwhile, just where the Northern sun
   Saluted first the Southern stone,
And Tuscan straw had lain a while,
   There sprang to light a flower unknown—

So wondrous fair, so vaguely sweet,
   One could not choose to pass it by,
That gay fair foreigner that came
   Where all was strange except the sky.

And now, from peasant's humble door
   To palace-gardens, everywhere,
That sunny bloom broadcast is seen
   That came unwittingly "with care."

And so, I think, when great events
   March grandly on, we creatures small
May comfort take, remembering
   "With care" is written over all.

THE DEACON'S TRIAL.

"I NEVER will forgive him—no;
   I'm mighty sure of that!"
So saying, Deacon Jacob Jones
   Took off his Sunday hat,
And smoothed it with his handkerchief,
   As he was wont to do,
Staring upon its faded shine
   As he would stare it through.

But, bless you! looking all the time,
   He never saw at all
The poor old beaver, as he went
   To leave it in the hall;
He only saw the handsome face
   Of Joe, the lawyer's son,
His rival at the polls to-day,
   Who had the office won.

"No, never will—no, Polly Ann;
   He had no call to try
Against me.—Had he, daughter Lu?
   Don't shake your curls and sigh!
A great six-footer, strong and well,
   Against me, old and lame,
And poor besides!—No, Polly Ann;
   It is a burning shame!"

"But, father"—then the bonny curls
   Swept on his homespun knee—
"Joe wanted it, because—because
   He wants to marry me,
And take you both with us to live."
   The deacon never stirred;
The kitchen clock went ticking on,
   The kitten slept and purred,

And Polly Ann stepped back behind,
   To say a word or two:
"Such feelin's, Jacob, isn't right,
   An' Sunday comin' too!

If our Josiah had a-lived
  He'd been as old as Joe,
And looked jest like him, wouldn't he?"
  The deacon muttered, "I don't know."

But put his old bandanna up
  Across his nose and eyes,
And wondered if the baby lost
  Grew up in Paradise.
Then, though there was no rush of wings,
  No shine of garments white,
A loving spirit hither stole
  To help him wrestle right;

For softly fell his clumsy hand
  On Lulu's bended head.
"I was a leetle hard on Joe;"
  These were the words he said.
But well they knew his dear old heart
  Had then and there forgiven,
And, unashamed, the angel took
  The record back to heaven.

THE SPIRIT'S JOURNEY TO DREAM-LAND.

SHUT close, white lids, lie quiet now,
  Bind poppy-blossoms on the brow;
So may I leave thee all alone,
Poor body, which I call my own.

Lie folded, hands, you've naught to do,
My journey has no need of you;
No gathered raiment seeks the soul,
For Dream-land gives its own white stole.

Poor patient face, with lines of care;
Poor faded cheek and tarnished hair;
Poor weary fingers, laid at rest
Over the quiet beating breast,

Poor tired feet, that stumble so
Along the path they seek to go,—
Lie still, poor body, silence keep,
Rocked in the gentle arms of sleep,

While I, thy soul, go flitting far,
Bound by no verge, held by no star,
Catching the skirts of angels gone
To ask why I am left alone.

I'll look in Youth's forgotten face,
And your remembered image trace;
Then summon, as I choose, to me,
Each form beloved I used to see.

And when they speak, as speak they must,
With speech untaught of human dust,
I'll tell thee, waking, what they say
Of deathless love that lives to-day.

And so, when morning blushes sweet,
Quicker shall go the patient feet,

More golden glow Life's ebbing sand,
With light I bring from Dreamer's Land.

A DISCONTENTED LEAF.

DID you ever hear of the Maple-leaf,
    His life full of discontent,
Grumbling through every day he lived,
    Growling wherever he went?

He found himself in the early spring
    Just out from a varnished crown,
And felt aggrieved at the shelter torn,
    And pushed it in anger down.

He quarrelled first with his lowly lot,
    Quite down on the great green tree,
And then at the crowd of leaves above
    As far as his glance could see.

He made complaint to the Forest Lord
    Regarding his verdant guise,
While tulips shone in the garden near
    With crimson and scarlet dyes.

Then straightway under the autumn sun
    He shone like a blossom gay;
Was he happy then in his new attire,
    Made of sunset colors? Nay.

He thought it an uneventful life
   Thus tied to a single tree;
He envied birds, going to and fro,
   And fish, swimming merrily.

"O restless one!" said the patient Lord,
   "Once more I will grant thy will."
So the severed leaf on a wild wind went
   Over meadow and vale and hill,

Flitting to and fro like a yellow bird,
   With a tinge of blood on its breast;
But he grumbled sore at his busy life,
   And clamored for idle rest.

"O fitful leaf!" said the Forest Lord,
   "Thou shalt know neither peace nor calm,
Till I lay thee down in thy last repose
   In sound of the forest psalm.

"Seize him and bind him, ye Sprites of Air,
   Pin him with snow-flakes down,
Over the bed where the crocus sleeps,
   Under its coverlet brown.

"Thus he shall shelter the patient ones
   Who wait as the good Lord wills,
Who question not what His wisdom does
   Under shadow of seeming ills."

THE CHRISTMAS SHEAF.

THERE was pitiful, querulous chirping
  Of snow-birds astir in the tree,
Which Winter Wind kindly translated,
  And whistled in rhythm to me.

"O mother-bird dear, we are hungry,
  Your poor, weary nestlings are faint;
How is it, O mother-bird, darling,
  You chirrup no sound of complaint?"

"My birdlings, away in the forest,
  Where searching for food had been vain,
I crouched in my desolate sorrow
  To murmur and chide and complain.

"Just then came a little brown singer,
  That hopped on the twig at my side,
And for answer to me and my wailing
  She chirruped, 'The Lord will provide.'

"'I see no provision,' I murmured;
  'The fruits are all gathered and gone,
The grain has been reaped in the valley,
  The frost nightly silvers the lawn.

"'So, patient one, how can He feed us,
  Since beautiful summer has died?'
And still she sang softly for answer
  This burden, 'The Lord will provide.'

"Then flying on, wearily homeward,
  With wings slowly beating the air,
I pondered the sweet lesson over,
  And sought better trust in His care.

"Then lo! on the barn-gable yonder,
  Where dwelleth good Ulric the Swede,
I saw the great wheat-sheaf uplifted
  That Northmen bestow on our need."

When Christmas its beautiful story
  Repeats from the bells far and nigh,
The birds of the air, unforgotten,
  Draw near to their banquet on high.

We'll sing, as we go, our thanksgiving,
  We'll try, as we never have tried,
To remember the wood-singer's lesson,
  And trust to the Lord to provide.

A LOST SUMMER.

HAS any one seen a lost summer,
  Strayed, stolen, or otherwise gone,
First missed when the leaves of September,
  Turned, showed us a frost-graven dawn?
And now she has hidden in frolic
  Beneath the low-lying, bright leaves.
Has any one seen a lost summer
  Afield with the banded corn-sheaves?

Not mine, with its true-hearted roses,
    Whose petals, shrunk sadly, yet sweet,
Bear incense from kerchief and ribbon
    As they flutter away to my feet;
Not mine, with its thankful remembrance
    Of all that I count and keep—
The grass on the hillside unbroken,
    The mercies of waking and sleep.

But I heard Kitty Avenue's mother,
    Through treacherous, close-folded blind,
As she strapped the last trunk, high and mighty,
    With Kitty's bright finery lined,
Discourse in no soft, measured accents,
    Till it seemed it was certainly so,
That the summer was lost when the damsel
    Had failed to secure a rich beau.

As she chided, the rows on the river
    With Allenby Lyle all alone,
And sundry piazza-spent evenings
    That projects and plans had o'erthrown,
Summing up, with a querulous quaver,
    Fair Kitty's "best season" as "lost,"
With a dreary remembrance upon her
    Of what the experiment cost.

"There was young Lamoureux nearly crazy,
    He's got a town-house and a yacht!
Old muddle-head Golden was raving
    About your blue eyes, and all that;

Then you snubbed Alexander Von Stiner—
  So provoking— Well, all I can say,
You can blame your own self, you remember;
  You've thrown your best season away."

O beautiful, low-lying summer!
  Peep over the hills of the South,
To whisper "not lost" to the matron,
  And spare the young tremulous mouth
That is shaping its newly-formed story,
  Albeit 'tis love in a cot,
Pressing hard on maternal ambition,
  That counts it a wearisome lot.

*   *   *   *

And then came the stir of departure,
  When, fair 'neath the wide gypsy hat,
I saw the sweet face of the culprit,
  The bonny blue eyes, "and all that,"
Heard the ripples of soft, merry laughter
  Well out from the girl's happy soul;
Ah! she carried her summer-time with her,
  Nor grudged Love the season he stole.

JOHN GRAY, JUNIOR.

UNDER a cloud of cradle-lace
  Nestled a tiny stranger face,
Thrice welcome to the failing race
      Of John Gray, Senior.

JOHN GRAY, JUNIOR.

Three times three the sunshine red
Looked through the curtains o'er its head,
To ask how time with Baby sped—
        With John Gray, Junior.

Thrice softly glided past the shade
Above a grave-rift, newly made,
To whisper where its mother laid.
        Poor John Gray, Junior!

And thrice three times a tutored step
Had softly to the cradle crept
To watch the stranger as he slept,
        Wee John Gray, Junior.

There as he took the tiny fist
Within his hand, and softly kissed
Its palm, there rose a shapely mist
        Round John Gray, Senior,

Of childhood bright, of school-days done,
Of college honors fairly won,
And by and by "John Gray and Son,"
        Senior and Junior.

The while a pitying angel knew
That ere the morning drank the dew
Life had been lived its limits through
        For John Gray, Junior.

    *   *   *   *

There were white roses everywhere,
Sweet flower-odors faint and fair

Around the waxen image there
        Of John Gray, Junior.

The sun came, as he used to do,
His golden hair flung streaming through
The blind, to say a long "adieu"
        To John Gray, Junior,

Then left the silent, shaded room
For ever to its purple gloom,
To gild the daisies on the tomb
        Of John Gray, Junior.

Low all the airy castles lie,
While tender hands lay softly by
The garments made so carefully
        For John Gray, Junior.

Now the small hand the father kissed
For ever beckons through the mist
That lies between yon world and this,
        For John Gray, Senior.

MABEL'S MISSION.

FAR down in the shady old garden,
  Where shadows are gathered to die,
On the myrtle, down-trodden, knelt Mabel,
  With face lifted up to the sky.

The bird in the maple was quiet,
  Looking down on the fair little maid,
And listened in decorous silence,
  While fervently thus Mabel prayed:

"More work for these too-idle fingers;
  More work for the body and brain,—
Some task for this God-given spirit;
  Some goal to be entered through pain,
Far out on the wide burning desert,
  Away over mountain and sea;
Oh show me, Lord, truly my mission—
  Some path that will lead me to Thee."

The bird heard the prayer, full of wonder;
  He knew of the sorrows and cares
That clustered the home-shadows under,
  Unheeded and trifling affairs.
No shine on the commonplace duty,
  To tell it was known up above;
No sign of a saintship in waiting
  For Patience and hard-tested Love.

Two mother-hands nerveless and weary,
  Unable their burdens to bear,
As they waver and tremble and falter
  Beneath the high pressure of care;
While Freddy, poor pain-smitten darling!
  Breathes gently a pitiful moan,
And waits in the gathering shadow
  The while, in his suffering alone.

And grandfather's queer childish fancies,
    Unwatched, lead to fearful mishap;
Grandmother finds real discomfort
    In crumples in kerchief and cap;
Poor Jack, fighting terrible fractions,
    The school-boy's implacable foe,
Calls loudly for Mabel. She listens,
    And straightway her temples lie low.

Oh see at your feet, little Mabel,
    Yon path winding up to yon door!
Oh seek in the isles of the ocean
    For God-given duties no more!
In the quiet home-lighted horizon
    You bound with the sound of a hymn,
Go garner the sheaf of the present;
    The duties beyond it are dim.

A QUESTION.

PRAY, may I ask you, country-lad,
    Whose smile no care can smother,
Tho' busy life throbs round about,
    "Have you written home to mother?"

You are forgetting, aren't you, quite
    How fast the weeks went flying,
And that a little blotted sheet
    Unanswered still is lying?

A QUESTION.

Don't you remember how she stood
   With wistful glance at parting?
Don't you remember how the tears
   Were in her soft eyes starting?

Have you forgotten how her arm
   Stole round you to caress you?
Have you forgotten those low words,
   "Good-bye, my son; God bless you!"

Have evil words dulled honest truth?
   Does homely love seem idle?
And playbills lie quite undisturbed
   Above the little Bible,

Until you have no heart to write,
   Can tell no pleasant story
Of steadfast feet that keep the way
   That leads at last to glory?

Oh, do not wrong her patient love;
   Save God's, there is no other
So faithful through all mists of sin—
   Fear not to write to mother.

Tell her how hard it is to walk
   As walked the Master lowly;
Tell her how hard it is to keep
   A man's life pure and holy.

Tell her to keep the lamp of prayer
   Alight—a beacon burning,

Whose beams shall reach you far away,
    Shall lure your soul returning.

Tell her you love her dearly still,
    For fear some sad to-morrow
Shall bear away the list'ning soul,
    And leave you lost in sorrow.

And then, through bitter, falling tears,
    And sighs you may not smother,
You will remember, when too late,
    You did not write to mother.

EVEN MEASURE.

"THIS very fine gentleman—what does he mean,
    With his loitering feet and his little white hands,
Watching me gearing these pulleys and bands,
And greasin' the wheels of this rattlin' machine?

"Hark! 'Labor is prayer.' Eh! what does he know
    Of the one or the other? I guess they are few—
    Them prayers and that preachin'. Sich talkin' won't do.
It's all very well for a man to talk so

"Who has holidays plenty, and money to spend,
    Not grimy like me from my head to my foot,
    Not choking with file-dust and cinders and soot,
With never a day when the battle will end.

"There's the noon-bell. There's Susy! I see her bright eyes,
 And her long yellow curls in the sun at the door;
 Bless her heart! if the lassie had been here before
I wouldn't have grumbled so. I wasn't wise.

"She loves her poor daddy in spite of his grime,
 And I'll wash my old face for my little girl's sake.
 There!—Noon, is it, Susy? The kiss now I'll take:
Daddy waits for a kiss when it comes dinner-time.

"Stranger, this is my gal—six years, going seven."
 The stranger looked up; his eye dimmer grew,
 And he spoke very softly: "I had a girl too,
But she went to the angels above us in heaven;

"And if I could buy her sweet company here
 By a life full of labor and care, as your own,
 I would work without measure, or murmur, or moan,
For the sake of the blessing I counted so dear."

"Well, stranger, yer pardon. I thought in my soul
 You never knew trouble, or sorrow, or care,
 And so I was frettin' inside, at yer fare
And my lot. Guess it's square on the whole."

BLOOM ABOVE, AND LABOR UNDER.

JUST beyond the line of faces,
   All along the city car,
Lo! I saw a florist's triumph,
   Made of blossom, bell and star—

Saw a fairy temple woven,
   From which triple baskets hung:
Red and white and azure clusters,
   Through, and under, tendrils swung.

Fuchsias drooped, a fringe of scarlet,
   Geraniums clung round about,
Begonia leaves with velvet shadows
   Threw each tender tinting out.

In among the twining greenness,
   Clasping close the fragile stand,
Just beneath the fairy roofing
   Saw I too a mournful hand—

Boyish, red, and rough and dingy,
   Thrust beyond a ragged sleeve,
Telling me its owner's story,
   Quite without its owner's leave.

Ragged sleeve said, "Motherless;"
   Grime and grace said, "Youth and trade."
Slender wrist and fingers whispered,
   "Born for sword, but doomed to spade."

Strangely out of place its roughness
  Showed beside the blossoms gay;
Bloom above, and labor under—
  'Tis the world's old-fashioned way.

And the lovely idle lilies,
  Born aristocrats, remain,
While the plodding human toiler
  Plucks his guerdon out of pain.

A SHINING LINK.

A FLECK of light on the psalm-book shone,
    And it quivered slow,
    Beating to and fro
With a quicker throb than the organ's tone.

Not the sun's own ray, for I faced the west,
    And the ruddy glare
    Of his sunset stare
Crept even now over brow and breast,

Nodding up and down as if answ'ring "Yes,"
    Or more softly stirred
    By the preacher's word,
When he spake of the Master's might to bless;

Or under his solemnly searching thought,
    Gliding to and fro,

As it answered "No"
To the "ought not" done, and the undone "ought."

Still watching this, I became perplexed,
    As the eerie thing
    Kept its steady swing,
Till I heard no longer the psalm or text.

When turning softly aside at last
    To the rich man's pew,
    All at once I knew
From whence the will-o'-the-wisp was cast.

For a diamond shone in the shaking ear
    Of a palsied dame,
    Like a living flame
Prisoned for ever within a tear.

Anew I watched with a deeper care,
    Praying One to bless,
    When it nodded "Yes"
To the echoed cry of the sinner's prayer.

Asking strength from Him for the poor old dame,
    When the light said "Nay"
    In its strange wise way,
As the preacher spake of the creature's claim.

So up to the edge of my book it crept,
    Like an elfin light,
    Until out of sight
The pendent spark in the tear unwept.

When homeward each through the twilight sped,
    Only God and I
    Knew the shining tie
From pitying heart to the palsied head.

THE POSTMAN OF THE AIR.

HOME to the quiet belfry,
    Oh haste thee, faithful dove!
Carry thy message safely,
    Brief words of war or love.

Over the vineyard wasted,
    Over the smoking town;
Over the army's glitter,
    Over the tarnished crown;

O'er the beleaguered city
    Lower thy dusky breast
Until its gold is shadow,
    Its beating turmoil, rest.

Under thy weary pinion
    Comfort and courage wait;
God guide thee, gentle postman,
    Within the guarded gate!

Keep thee through airy perils—
    From falcon swift and sure;
From cruel beating tempest,
    From fowler's cunning lure.

Go tell the gallant soldier
   Where lies the hidden foe,
Where flaunts the hostile banner,
   Where ambush crouches low.

Bring from the banished mother,
   A blessing for her son,
And from the bride, remembrance
   To the beloved one.

Thus, spite of man's invention,
   "Sought out" through ages past,
To thee, frail postal angel,
   He comes for help at last—

Back to the gentle story
   Of homesick birds afar;
So peace belies her emblem
   Beneath the cloud of war.

WOMAN'S KINGDOM.

"WOMAN'S kingdom!" Who knows where
   The walls of woman's kingdom are?
How stands her throne in purple state,
Gemmed with the golden bees of Fate?
Where is her crown of glory won,
Her regal robes for pageants spun?
When may the warders dare to sleep
Beside the dungeon in the keep?

What is the tribute vassals pay,
And when the solemn reck'ning-day?
How are its courtly phrases learned,
And jewelled orders hardly earned?

Not where rude wassail, loud and deep,
Wakens the warder if he sleep;
Not where the vassal proffers gold,
Or love with priestly rite is sold;
Not where the garment's golden sheen
Shows jewelled ribbon broad between;
Not where the polished precepts taught
In silver accents, count for naught;
Not there her kingdom.
                    Reaching high,
Its walls rise upward to the sky,
For weary souls who crave her aid,
For frightened souls sin-sick, afraid,
While she beside the postern stands
To hold up weak and weary hands.

Her throne—the hallowed chamber where
Her child is taught its evening prayer;
Her crown—a good man's steadfast love,
Pure gold that fire shall only prove;
Her warders—only loving prayers
To guard the feet of stumbling cares;
Her tribute—loving hearts and true;
Her orders, Faith's broad ribbon blue,
Decked with the cross and starry Hope,
Borne on a shining anchor up.

This, this is woman's kingdom, left
When Paradise was from her reft.

PARIS FASHIONS.—(WAR TIME.)

"WHAT is the mode in Paris?"
  What is the latest style?
Where has the changeful goddess
  Hidden herself the while?

Not with the Señoritas,
  Changeless in veil and fan;
Not in the British Islands,
  Or warring Allemand.

Not in the Switzer valleys,
  Or chained by the Russian bear;
A homeless vagrant only,
  She wanders everywhere.

* * *

I'll tell you the Paris fashions,
  As well as a Yankee may:
There's a gun and knapsack ready
  For the red of a coming day.

There's a royal Yankee fashion
  That we sent to them over sea,
With the Stars and Stripes for trimming,
  And the Cap of Liberty.

There's a style of cutting yonder
  That wounded the Dryads sore,
For the ancient wood lies level
  With the sunshine on its floor.

There's a new mail-route from Paris,
  And the highway is the air,
Where the cloudy track is hidden,
  And the offices—anywhere.

There's a grim old fashion yonder
  Of "the useless mouths outside,"
Of a weeping, helpless army—
  Mother and child and bride.

And, saddest of all old fashions
  That clings to the tumbled nest,
Is the stain of the Godless Sabbath,
  By the smile of its King unblessed.

While yonder a terrible fashion
  Looks over the "arrowy Rhine,"
For the red on its floating garments
  Is of heart-blood, and not of wine.

So these are the Paris fashions,
  And this is her life to-day,
While the queen is a homeless vagrant,
  And the court like a vanished day.

OVER THE LAKE.

OVER the lake lies a silver mist,
The last good-bye of the sunset kissed,
Trailing its veil on the line of blue,
O far-off home, nearer me, than you!

Blithe little waves, as they run ashore,
Babble of faces I see no more;
While over them all, with oars adrip,
A boat comes in from a fairy ship.

A fairy craft that awaits no tide,
I call at will from the other side,
To leave the breath of the far salt sea,
With cargo marked and consigned to me.

Dear eyes there are on its deck ashine,
Warm hands I clasp, as I used, in mine;
Low, gentle words by the firelight said,
And tender tears for the early dead—

Sunshiny places, where Life and I
Laid care and sorrow and sighing by,
Where light and love and the summer, made
Green islands bright in a sea of shade.

These are the treasures upon her deck;
No storm can shatter or typhoon wreck;
This is the ship that I wait to see
Sailing, still sailing, in shore to me.

So when I stop at the blue lake's bound,
The wave comes up like a stranger hound,
And touches me with its tawny foot,
Where still I stand on the pebbles mute,

Looking across at the line of blue
That lies, dear home, nearer me than you,
Then runs aside, while the ripples say,
"She waits her shadowy ship to-day."

RUTH AND LOT.

"'OH, that's the old maid.' Are they talkin' of me?
I s'pose I am one, fur I'm nigh forty-three,
And I seem like a hundred, I s'pose, to the girls,
With my sober brown suit and these little gray curls.
But I kinder forgit till I hear it. It's true,
And I am an old maid. I git kinder blue;
Only sent fur to fun'rals, an' quiltin's, and teas;
Settin' up with sick creeturs to watch if they sneeze,
An' nobody thinkin' how lonesome I am.
There's the motherless children, be sure, and there's Sam,
The prince of good brothers; but sometimes I guess
They could live on without me. Old cat, I confess
I've a poor foolish streak in my heart—don't you tell—
An' I wish I'd made up, after pouting a spell,

With that Lot. What a bright eye he had!
What a pair of square shoulders, the great loving
    lad!
An'—listen, old cat, as you look in the fire—
He thought I was favorin' Abner the squire;
But I wasn't at all. Ah! well, let it go;
I'm a lonesome old maid—I must think of it so.
But when the girls' lovers hang over the gate,
An' Sammy keeps sayin', 'Them fellers stays late,'
I say, 'Oh, it's early,' to help them. I know,
An' I haven't forgotten, how such minutes go.
They say Lot is travellin'. Sam says he is gray
As a rat—Sammy heard of him over the way—
But I s'pose, if I saw him, he wouldn't know
    me.—
Well, Sammy, what is it? Why, what can it be?"
"A big letter, Ruthie—a man's writin' too.
Why, Ruthie, you're blushin', an' ain't read it
    through!
There now! it's a widower comin', I know.—
Eh, children, we'll never let Aunt Ruthie go;
Will we, chickies?"—"No, never; we'll kill him,
    Aunt Ruth."—
"Why, children, I b'lieve that I hit on the truth,
For I saw Lot McCurdy to-day in the town,
An' he looked kind o' queer.—Why, where has
    Ruth gone?"

    *   *   *   *   *

What the long letter said, you and I'll never
    know;
It was something, I guess, all about long ago.

And there's wailing at Sam's, and the cat's gone
    away,
And a big country-house has a mistress to-day;
So I fancy that Sammy had hit on the truth,
And the quarrel was ended between Lot and Ruth.

BESIDE A FAIRY FIRE.

IF Christmas-time could only seem
    As it used to do, lang syne;
If one could keep their dreams, awake;
If beaded bubbles would not break
    Over the ebbing wine;

If one could hear in fancy now
    The reindeer on the roof,
And know the merry nearing clank
Beside a stocking long and lank
    Would stop for our behoof;

If one could tiptoe out of bed
    With such a lightsome heart,
To find some jolly, kindly saint,
In memory of legend quaint,
    Once more had done his part;

If one could hang a stocking now
    Beside some fairy fire,

Creeping like childhood off at night,
And like it finding with the light
   Each darling wish, each dear desire

To find the silver star of Hope,
   For us to wear alway;
Hearts that we covet for our own,
The promised white and mystic stone,
   The lamp to guide us in the way;

The cloak that charity bestows;
   The glad youth that is gone;
A letter from the shining shore,
From happy ones gone on before,
   To help us struggle on;—

Ah! then we'd hang our stockings up,
   As well as Lou and Ben;
And if they were not full at first—
So full the gaping stitches burst—
   We'd hang them up again.

TEDDY'S LETTER.

WHAT a harmless thing intirely,
   Wid its writin' all agee,
Looks this bit of letter, comin'
   From old Ireland here to me!

But I tell you tears is startin',
   An I'm chokin' as I go

(I can read but very poorly),
   But the words hit like a blow.

Gone for ever, mother darlint!
   Gone widout one word fur me,
To tell me you'd forgiven Teddy!
   Gone, for ever! woe is me!

Can't I see your eyes a-shinin'
   In the darkened cabin-door,
When I turned away in anger,
   'Cause you scolded when I swore?

Backward turnin' at the corner,
   Lookin' when you couldn't see,
Wipin' tears off wid your apron—
   Bitter tears that fell fur me.

So I left you in my anger,
   Sailed that night from home and you,
Yet I see you cryin' softly
   Tears upon your apron blue.

Gathered pounds I jest was keepin',
   Jest was fixin' up a home,
Jest was meanin' to write humbly
   I was sorry—would ye come?

I'll read it over. What's this linin',
   Done by John? "Our mother said,
'Tell my Teddy I forgave him,
   Loved him alway—darlin' Ted!'"

Jest before she came to sunrise—
  Now, it seems, as I can see
Mother lookin' out o' glory,
  Smilin' softly down at me!

HERE AND THERE.

"SEE! the birds are here!" "Ah! the birds have
      gone!"
One cry o'er another slips,
Till adown in the tangled beaten grass
  The foot of the summer trips.

All the rosy wreaths of the May-buds lie
  Under brown September sheaves,
While across the top of the empty nest
  Arachne her kerchief weaves.

"The birds have come!" Did they ever sing,
  Little Ruth, so sweet before?
Listen long and well, for the song to-day
  Is a song without encore.

The birds will come with another spring,
  And the May-bush blossoms show;
But the sweetest song they can sing but once—
  But once can the same rose blow.

"Ah! the birds have gone!" Nay, the maid be-
    trothed
  Cares not for the empty nest;

For the sunny time touching now and then
   Holds within a lover-guest.

So they faintly call from the August edge
   Of summer to say, "Good-bye,"
But she never misses the singing band
   That fades in the southern sky;

For the happy time that was strangely short
   'Twixt coming and going wings
Had its own fair idyl rhymed and set,
   And this, little Ruthie sings.

"See! the birds are here!" "Lo! the birds have
     gone!"
   Ah! in all your lifetime, dear,
They will never sing, never once again,
   As they sang, little Ruth, this year.

THE LAST LETTER.

WHO knows when the *last* letter comes
   How tender and touching a sorrow
May hang o'er the commonplace words
   The postman shall bring with the morrow!

A little white fluttering fold,
   It tells not its terrible story;
Nor whispers 'neath ripples of speech
   Its place in the doorway of glory.

We read it, mayhap with a smile,
　　Then toss it by idly, undreaming
That, rescued, we'll scan it again
　　With glances through bitter rain streaming.

Its chance words of tenderness then
　　Like gold from the mass shall be sifted;
The speech of our ev'ry-day life
　　Into grandeur and greatness be lifted.

All harshness shall fold itself down,
　　As the calyx shrinks under the flower;
All blemishes vanish and fade
　　In the loving regrets of that hour.

The last little blossom dropped out
　　From the hand on the bank of the river,
Shall tell from its petals adroop
　　Sweet stories of love from the giver.

THE TUBEROSE.

O FLAGONS of odor set!
　　Pour draughts of your summer wine;
Come rock on my heart a while,
　　Fair stars on the earth ashine.
I've loved languid lilies well,
　　Have gathered red roses sweet,
Upreached for laburnum gold,
　　Plucked clover about my feet;

But they have no word for me,
  No speech in their scented sprays,
Save only a dimming dream
  Of the sun-lighted summer days.
But thou in my braided hair
  Out-shimmered one pale moonlight,
And so the sweet tale of love
  Seems linked with thy beauty white.
O glorious, gladsome life
  That over and round me glows!
This pleasure I have to keep,
  The breath of the tuberose.

  * * * *

Have you ever known what it was to droop
  At the breath of the tuberose—
To shrink from the gusts of its warm perfume,
  As you would from unfriendly blows—
To turn aside from its waxen stars,
  And shudder your wet lids down,
With an aching heart for the part it bore
  In a funereal cross and crown—
To trace with its petals so fair and white
  The unanswered name you call,
And circle the beautiful still white stars
  On the midnight gloomy pall?
Oh give me, to gather, the bright red rose,
  The laburnum and clover bloom,
Great golden lilies and asters gay!
  They tell no tale of a tomb.

O solemn shadow! and is this life,
  Where the haunted buds unclose,
And the very casket around our dead
  May unlock with a tuberose?

JOHN ELIOT, THE INDIAN APOSTLE.

SAILING on to a New World harbor,
  Sailing near—up to Boston town—
The good ship Lyon dropped her anchor,
Marked with the sign of the British crown.
What merchandise she safely carried
Over the dark November sea
It matters not;
            Her human freighting
Is calling still to you and me.

Back from the Mayflower's keel the ripple,
Chiming sweet to a waiting band,
Lured them too to the open temples
God had built in the Pilgrims' land;
Waiting wives and betrothèd maidens
Came as the bird's mate heeds its call;
Christian preachers and stalwart soldiers
Slipped from the Old World's bitter thrall.

Eager eyes, full of wistful wonder,
Longing looked to the nearing town,
Over the hilltop's azure shadow,
Over the woodland dim and brown.

Winthrop's wife, and his rosy children,
Sought the deck as they nearer drew;
For husband and father waited yonder,
Over the less'ning stretch of blue.

Outlooking stood the English teacher,
John Eliot. He did not know
He saw his kingdom stretched before him,
His crown beneath New England's snow.
Ah! how my pulse leaps to remember
More than two hundred years have gone,
And still within this wrist-vein purple
That blessed Pilgrim blood flows on!

*   *   *   *

We turn the leaves of the good man's life
Till we pass a score of years,
And a pictured page of his blessed work
Lies over its hopes and fears.

Fair, gentle Anne in her English home
But waited the builded nest,
Then came, troth-plighted long ago,
To the English teacher's breast;
Who, long ago, being ill content
With the care of a parish wide,
With hungry heart, looking still about
For the waiting souls outside,
Through the darkened door of a language new
Had gone like a palmer gray,

With the staff of prayer and its scallop shell,
Till he came to the open day.

And now we pause at the good man's side
As he touches his earthly crown
Where Natick stands:
                "The place of hills,"
The Indian's Christian town.
The drum-beat sounds; 'tis sermon-time:
From the wigwams far and near
Gather dusky forms to the preacher's side,
Of the grand New Trail to hear.
They gather in to the rounded fort,
To the house their hands have made,
With its "prophet's chamber" up above,
Its fittings in order laid.

From the "Bay State Psalm-Book's" open page
Reads Monequessun,* line by line,
A glad triumphant song of praise
That thrills o'er the list'ning pine,
Until the forests of Natick ring
With the song of Love Divine.
Then, lifting upward the busy hands
That garnered this harvest in
From the dusky aisles of the wilderness,
From its sullen gloom of sin,
The good Apostle, in words they know,
Of the "hidden treasure" tells,
And still on pardon, mercy, grace,
With a loving accent dwells—

        * The Indian reader.

Still thanking Him that the copper coin
Of the Master's realm should be
Redeemed, and in His image cast,
Through his mercy wide and free.

Ah! faithful one, that open door
"Cleare sunshine"* through it shows;
The wilderness has awaked to song,
And the desert found her rose.

*   *   *   *

Once more we stand by our kinsman's side,
Drawing nearer to Beulah's gate,
In his patient way asking only help
For his call from the King to wait.
A year ago, faithful Anne went on,
And the saint has been heard to say,
"That the friends beloved gone on before
Would fear he had missed the way."

More than fourscore years his head have bowed;
The pilgrim is waiting there,
And he sits with his idle folded hands
At rest, in his study-chair.
His feet no more in the wilderness
For the wandering sheep may stray,
But the far outreaching thrill of prayer
Farther runs than his step, to-day.

His hands still proffer his open purse,
That needs neither tie nor rings;

* Title of an old book in reference to his work.

For the whisper soft of Charity
Will loosen its tightest strings.
His busy pen hath no record made
Of his worldly gain or loss;
But through a language its point has ploughed,
Till it came to the planted Cross.

Softly and tenderly bending down
His head on his Master's breast,
With the parting whisper, "Welcome, joy!"
He sinks to his heavenly rest.
The echoes soft of the near response
We hear through the parted cloud,
As he lays his work at his Master's feet,
While the angels nearer crowd.

    *   *   *   *

They laid him down in the quiet shade
Of the church he had loved so well,
When the busy robins came to build,
And the May-blooms o'er him fell;
No word of praise o'er his ashes speaks,
For the motto—yours and mine—
"Occurrent nubes," loses truth
As he stands in the "cleare sunshine."

HYMN.

"We give Thee hearty thanks for the good examples of all those Thy servants, who, having finished their course in faith, do now rest from their labors."

WE praise Thee, God, the Pilgrim's stay,
    Whose hand supports Thy people still,
Since first the sea became a path
    Beneath the footsteps of Thy will—

A silver link from shore to shore,
    By true Evangel safely crossed,
Held fast by prayer at either end,
    Tho' shaken sore and tempest-tossed.

We bless Thee for the solemn psalm
    That stirred the forest arches then,
Whose echoes, ringing down the years,
    Still blend to-day with our Amen.

We thank Thee for our common sire,
    God's freeman, by the truth made free,
A lineage more blest by far
    Than kingly line could ever be.

So teach his children's children still
    To walk as wisely as he trod,
And, thanking Thee for Pilgrim sire,
    Help us to trust the Pilgrim's God.

DINNERS AND DARNS.

'TIS a wearisome, work-a-day world,
  Made of dinners, and duties, and darns;
Ah, if one could be kept like the birds,
  Needing not either storehouse or barns;
To be looking for dust on the stairs,
  When the woods have their blossoming floors;
To be stitching at gathers and hems,
  When the world is abloom out of doors;
To be treading the round of each day,
  Leaving mountains and torrents unseen;
To be battling with spiders at home
  When the fern on the hillside is green!
No pageants move down the highway,
  Like the olden-time glorious sights,
Neither tournament, gallant and gay,
  Neither castles, nor heroes, nor knights;
No fair silken sleeve to be pinned
  On Sir Lancelot's shield as he rides;
No palmer goes wearily by,
  No minstrel, song-welcomed, abides.
And yet—am I right?—is it all?
  Only dinners and darns that we see?
Looking down on this work-a-day world,
  Is there not even yet chivalry?
Is there not in the care-woven thread,
  Deftly thrown by a woman's weak hand,
The deep pathos of Poverty's speech,
  Or the rooting of Honesty grand?

What knight riding down the long age,
    With a blazon ashine on his crest,
Ever fought such a foe as the man
    Who hath smitten a sin from his breast?
Nay, what of earth's beautiful sights,
    Mighty torrent or hill's misty crest,
Shall be better to see, from above,
    Than a mother-bird rounding her nest?

THE TREE OF YOUTH.

HEARD you of the tale of Ibor,
    Mussulman and traveller old,
Who such strange, fantastic story
    Hath in ancient volume told,

Of the leaves for Youth's renewal
    Falling from the cypress tree,
Of its close concentric pathways
    Trodden bare by devotee?

Where the sun of Ceylon brightens
    Palm and river, shore and steep,
Till its golden tissue tangles
    In the drowsy thicket's sleep,

High, among the tropic leafage,
    Spring the crown and column fair
Of the mystic, fateful cypress
    To the golden upper air.

Close beneath, with failing footsteps,
    Eyes too dim to mark its crest,
Walk the aged, worn with waiting,
    Looking for the harvest blest;

For at times unknown, uncertain,
    Precious leaves are said to drop,
Potent for rejuvenescence,
    From the cypress' stately top.

Ah! if anywhere beyond us
    There should spring a tree so fair,
How the pilgrim throng would quicken
    On the well-worn pathway there!

How uplifted hands would struggle
    For one chance to try again,
Though the new lease be no better
    Than the old one with its pain!

ATTAINED.

A SHINING whorl of the fashioned frost
    With its silver petals lapped across
Was over the buried lilies tossed.

'Twas like a star in its saintly shine,
Or like a gem from a river-mine,
This snowy rose made of silver rime.

But deep in the frozen bosom set
Was a murmur low, full of deep regret
For the soul denied to the snow-bloom yet.

All vain its dower of petals white,
Its silver crown fretted fair and light,
That touched no heart with its beauty bright.

No kiss of love to its shimmer bent,
No loving form o'er its fairness leant,
Till its little life had been lonely spent.

* * * *

A whisper rose from a lily-bell,
As it opened soft under April's spell,
"Oh listen, wind, till my joy I tell!

"I did but sleep for a little space;
My Master seemed but to hide his face,
To clasp me close in a new embrace—

"A little while in the silent tomb,
Ere I rose anew in a lily's bloom,
To light the shade of the garden's gloom.

"And now, through the blossom's velvet scroll,
I take, unbought, from His hand the dole
Of a lily's peaceful and sinless soul—

"A lily's soul with its message rare
For the passer-by, through the scented air,
With its kisses gathered everywhere."

GARLAND OR HAWSER.

JUST side by side, through the sunny weather,
   Two field-bouquets grew apace together;
They laughed alike with their bright blue eyes
On the open face of the summer skies;

Alike were wet in the falling dew,
As the moon dropped silver their shadows through;
And they bent alike to the summer rain,
Or smiled through tears at the sun again.

But the one was plucked by a lady fair,
On her bodice bound, in her amber hair,
While her dainty fingers their fibres wound,
Till the blossomed hemp was a garland bound.

And the other left, till the ripened crop,
Like a human thing, faded first atop,
And was roughly torn by a menial grasp
From the gentle Earth and her loving clasp.

Is the world at best but a lot unfair?
Here, a garland blooms in a woman's hair;
There, another lies under careless feet,
With its life, as we think it, incomplete.

    *   *   *   *   *

Driving in ashore comes a keel to-night,
And a rocket's flash lightens breakers white,
While a voice goes by on the wailing blast,
With a life-line out over darkness cast.

See! along the track of its fearful way
How the human hopes of a creature sway!
Heaven help thee, lad! struggle on once more;
There are stretched-out hands on the friendly shore.

Battle on with wind, husband well thy breath;
On a fraying rope trembles life or death!
For its strands are chafed in the rock-strewn sea,
Until one is cut, and there were but three!

Tighten, field-bouquet that the dew has kissed,
Like a band of-steel let thy fibres twist;
Heaven give thee strength till the lad comes through!
Ha! another cord!—and there were but two!

For your life, my lad! but a boat's length more!
But a breast-high wave! He has gained the shore,
Breathing thankful prayer. So its work was done.
And the lone strand cut and there was but one!

With a swift recoil to the depths below,
Then the rope went out with the undertow,
But a ripple sang through the sea-foam dim,
"Garland fair or hawser can work for Him."

THE LOST SKY.

I WISH I knew
    That the blessed blue
We have learned to call the sky
    Was a real dome
    Over this earth home,
Steadfast and strong and high.

    I would rather think
    Little stars that blink
Are hung in a strong roof sure
    By a tether fast,
    So a cloud swung past
Can no shining ship unmoor.

    I should like to feel
    That the sun's great wheel
Brushes close to the arching wall,
    And the shooting star
    Need not travel far
If it fears, at the last, to fall.

    Only ether blue
    Dimming through and through—
Nor a shore for a thought adrift,
    Not a spar to clutch,
    Not a line to touch,
Where the planets' white wings lift.

    Only pale air rolled,
    Till its misty fold

Glitters bright with an azure glow,
  With the stars strung through
  Like the pearls of dew,
On nothing that sight can know.

  But the mystic stair
  Of the rainbow fair,
With its shining footsteps seven,
  Comes not more near
  Than our stairways here
To our souls beloved in heaven.

  Ah! the pillars high
  Of my childish sky
I could reach with a childish thought;
  But a throb of pain
  Stirs the woman's brain,
For the truth to a woman taught.

CHARCOAL'S STORY.

I'M only Charcoal, the blacksmith's dog,
  Ugly, and fast growing old,
Lying in sunshine the livelong day,
  By the forge when the nights are cold.
I look across at the little house,
  The door where I used to wait
For a school-boy shout, a merry face
  To meet me within the gate.

My master, the smith, remembers too;
  I see on his grimy cheek,
As he looks across at the cottage-door,
  A pitiful tear-drawn streak.
He, stooping, lays in a trembling way
  His hand on my lifted head;
I look and whine, but we understand—
  Each thinks of the school-boy dead.

"Prince" is the tawny and handsome hound
  That comes with the hunting squire;
Smooth and well-fed, with a stable bed,
  And a place by the kitchen fire.
"The squire is going away," he said;
  He waited an hour to-day,
While master carefully shod his mare
  In his slow, old-fashioned way.

I heard him say, with an oath or two,
  "Put an end to that sorry cur;
Better buy my Prince—he's a noble beast."
  I heard, but I did not stir;
For I knew I was only a worn-out thing,
  Not bright like the tawny hound,
And I felt I would gladly go and die
  On a short new churchyard mound.

"Well, squire"—the strong arm rose and fell,
  The sparks from the anvil flew—
"I s'pose the critter that's lyin' there
  Is not much account to you;

But while I live, and can earn his keep,
   Old Charcoal and I won't part;
For, squire, I really think sometimes
   The dog has a human heart.

"My little Jacky—he loved him so—
   And Jacky he's gone, you see;
And so it 'pears as if Charcoal knows
   That he's more than folks to me."

The squire is gone with his horse and hound,
   And master and I still wait
Together, and side by side go in
   At night through the lonely gate;
But by and by one must go alone—
   One only be left of three,
To pass the gate and cottage-door:
   Alas! if it should be me!

THROUGH THE MIST.

THE cold white mist crept silently
   Up from the river's edge,
Hanging its curtain from the sky
   Down to the sodden sedge;
I could not see the ragged shine
   Of wavelets dancing fair,
But, though I saw no merry stream,
   I knew the stream was there.

I looked along the village street,
    Seeking the steeple white
Crowning the modest little kirk,
    But that had vanished quite;
From trodden sill to turret top
    No outline cut the air;
I could not see, but then I knew
    The little church was there.

I could not see the gladsome sun,
    Shadowless stood the tree—
Unbarred the path where streaks of light
    At morning used to be;
The sky no hint or token gave
    Of sunshine anywhere;
But tho' I could not see the sun,
    I knew the sun was there.

And thus I came to think at last
    How firm our trust should be
In things we count immutable,
    The while we may not see.
If God has willed that round about
    Shall rise the mists of care,
Till faith seems but a melting spire,
    I'll trust the church is there.

If cold unwelcome fogs arise
    To dim love's pleasant shine,
I'll wait and look beyond the mist
    Which this side gives no sign;

If light grows dim, and sunshine cold
Wrapped in earth's murky air,
I know the fault lies in the mist—
The faithful sun is there

CAMP-MEETING SUNDAY AT OCEAN GROVE.

FROM the bud of a cloud-calyxed midnight
Comes the bloom of the clear Sunday morn,
And the crown of the week, with hosannas
In sun-lighted beauty is born.

I sit in the shaded Pavilion
That centres these homes by the sea,
In the city whose name tells its story—
Fair child of the wave and the tree.

I see the oaks standing about me,
God's sentinels, steady and true,
Up-bearing their sky-rifted banners,
Where sunshine comes brokenly through.

I look up to pleasant roof-shadow,
Strong built, 'gainst the storm to defend
(It is good to look upward for shelter,
Still upward, for aye, to the end).

I see a blue line over yonder,
That sends a salt kiss on the breeze,
And the sound of the sea, chanting softly,
Comes echoing up to the trees.

A cloud, soft and snowy, floats upward;
　　I think, as I watch it flit o'er
Out of sight, 'tis the glorified body
　　Of the wavelet that died on the shore.

Around and about me, uncounted,
　　Throng worshippers, drifting together,
As the leaves in the hollows are heaped
　　By the gusts of the bright autumn weather—

Blooming girls, in the pride of their beauty;
　　Old men, with the almond-bloom crowned;
Pale and pitiful worn women's faces,
　　Where tear-drops a channel have found;

Stout men, with their hardened hands folded;
　　Fair children, whose song is a prayer;
And grandams, who wait to go over,
　　Full soon, to the "home over there."

Now, they glow as the hymn rises upward,
　　Now, bow 'neath a prayer-laden breath,
Now, a shout supplements the glad story
　　Of "ransomed from sin and from death."

Rising now, hark! they sing "Coronation,"
　　Sing of kingdom and glory to be,
Till the gates of the city stand open
　　To the surge of humanity's sea.

O beautiful Camp-meeting Sunday!
　　When clouds on my path hover low,

I shall call up thy happy remembrance
  To cheer me wherever I go.

And tho' in this sun-lighted temple
  I'll meet this great host never more,
We shall meet in the Lamb-lighted City,
  When the wave bears us up the bright shore.

A SUNDAY EVENING BEACH-SERVICE AT OCEAN GROVE.

THE tide is in, and the weary waves,
  That have come with their solemn story
Across the leagues, throw their white hands up
  In the light of the sunset glory.

Too weary now, from their journey long,
  To climb up the smooth sand sloping,
They falter back, as to gather strength,
  For a stronger impulse hoping.

Up and down the shore, seeking levels low,
  To be reached by a new endeavor,
They writhe and turn, in the white unrest
  God decreed to the waves for ever.

Closing down to the line of breakers white,
  See, another wave comes foaming—

BEACH-SERVICE AT OCEAN GROVE.

A seething surge of humanity
  To break by the seaside moaning.

Up and down the shore, from the tattered edge
  Of the ocean's silver shredded,
To the faint new moon and the little star
  On the low horizon threaded,

A living wave from the world's great sea,
  From its ceaseless, sad commotion,
Breaks with a song of praise and prayer
  On the sands of the solemn ocean.

And the dear old hymns that have cradled saints—
  Dear words that have been their pillow
To Jordan's edge, on the air ring out—
  Through the psalm of the beating billow.

Whilst the ruddy sunset burns and glows
  Till the gates ajar stand yonder,
And I hear a voice from the pulpit boat
  Chime in with the billow's thunder:

"After this I looked, and behold a door
  Was opened in heaven." The story
Six hundred voices bore along
  In the words of the dream of glory.

"And before the throne was a sea of glass
  Mingled with fire." Slow turning,
It seemed the shores of the crystal sea
  Were under the sunset burning.

So a solemn lull with the twilight fell,
    And the psalm in the sea-moan ended,
As the purple hush of the silent night
    On the scattered throng descended.

BETTER THAN DIAMONDS.

YES, I was the belle of the ball, mamma—
    Yes, I was the belle of the ball.
All the men bowed down at my feet, mamma,
    And the women they envied all.
But out in the wonderful solemn night,
    As I came from the revel gay,
How I felt rebuked by the holy stars
    And the gleam of the morning gray!

Oh what do the beautiful risen souls,
    And what do the angel-bands, think
Of the empty life of the butterfly
    As it flits on the torrent's brink?
I am sick at heart of it all, mamma,
    Tho' I was the belle of the ball,
For between the bars of the gayest waltz
    There re-echoed, "And is this all?"

Ah! nobody saw how an angel stooped
    Lower down with his drooping wings;
Human ears heard not the soft seraph speech
    As it whispered of heavenly things—

But a woman's soul at its turning stood,
   Tho' her answer was low and calm,
As she laid her humble and trusting soul
   In the scarred but puissant palm.

There were lonely homes in the far " out West,"
   Where the gaunt grim fingers of Care,
Heaping up the dust on the Bible-lids,
   So had smothered the Sabbath fair,
Until seed-time, and harvest, came and went
   With never a prayer or a cry,
Except when a coffin's dark shadow fell,
   Or the thunder came hurtling by.

Many lonely and stifled souls were there
   Who still kept in remembrance dear
Little humble churches their childhood knew,
   Sabbath bells that they used to hear—
Weak and weary saints, who had prayed so long
   Without answer, thought He forgot
Their Christian needs, as the harvests went by,
   And the churches and bells were not.

Truly, all the while, in the Master's time,
   Was the work for the Master done,
When the ballroom belle under starlight stood,
   All weary of worship won.
To the earnest cry of her wakened soul
   Followed swiftly a blest reply,
And the alchemy of an earnest heart
   Laid her jewels away on high.

When the shining cross she had worn that night
    O'er her weary, unquiet breast
Took a grander shape, as a prairie church
    In the midst of the wilderness;
The diamond drops that had graced her ears,
    Transformed, had good tidings to tell,
When the voices of grateful saints thanked God
    For the sound of the sweet church-bell.

Her gold, shod stronger and fleeter feet
    Than her own, for the King's highway,
And her little hands held an open purse
    Evermore for the pilgrims' stay.
When safely at last on life's upper stair
    She turned by the gateway near,
Lo! a shining cross glittered fair to see
    By the banks of the river clear.

There they sang together, the succored saints
    And the beautiful ballroom belle,
For each had the glowing redemption-song
    And the tale of His love to tell.
"Better than diamonds," echoed the harps—
    "Yes, better than diamonds far!"
So the shout rang out through the ransomed ranks,
    So repeated the morning star.

HOME FROM MEETING.

"NAY, mother, I fear not; the good Lord can keep us
  Through this, the bright, clear Sabbath day;
Little Avis and I will be home from the meeting
  Before the next twilight is gray."

"But, Reuben, the Pequods are murdering people!
  Think of Deerfield and dark Bloody Brook!"
And the mother who loved him drew nearer to Reuben,
  Though her limbs in their feebleness shook.

That winter had passed full of tumult and horror,
  Two centuries back of our time;
For the Indian arrow had written its story
  In the colony's record of crime.

There were stories of strange, lurid sights in the heavens,
  When comets were sharp, shining swords,
And pale, dancing lights of the mystic aurora
  Presaged coming of Indian hordes.

"Though a host should encamp round about me," said Reuben,
  "Though the redskins are out by the score,
I will go on to meet with His worshipping people,
  And pray my way up to the door."

"Then leave the child, Reuben—leave Avis in
    safety."
"Nay, mother, the God that I serve,
He is able to keep her, if such be His pleasure;
    Why, then, should I slacken or swerve?"

"Good-bye, and God bless you!" The aged eyes,
    watching
Through tears, saw the travellers start—
Watched their lessening forms out of sight down
    the valley,
    Till hills wedged their two lives apart.

What wonder the woman's heart failed in her
    bosom
    As she saw them not over the hill!
What wonder that fancies she could not exorcise
    Came round in the Sabbath day still!

The child, little Avis, the dead mother's darling,
    What if she should be smitten and slain?
Her tremulous hands pressed hardly her bosom,
    As those do who struggle with pain,

Till she fell on her knees by the worn Bible open,
    Glad refuge of souls sore afraid,
And out of the trust of a Puritan mother
    For the loved ones in danger she prayed:

"O God of my fathers, keep Reuben in safety!
    Put the arms of thy love round about!

Turn the arrows aside from the motherless maiden,
  Though the terrible Pequods are out!"

     *   *   *   *

And then—hours of watching, till lo, in the sunset
  Came a glimmer of gun-barrel bright;
And on, up the valley, thank God! slow and surely
  Came the twain into safety and sight.

"And the hound, Reuben?"—"Yonder, a mile or two back,
  With an arrow transfixed in his breast."—
"You have come out of danger?"—"Ay, mother, 'tis true;
  Little Avis will tell you the rest."

"Oh, grandmother dear, by the mill the horse shied,
  Carlo leaped with a terrible cry,
And I saw father clutch at his gun-barrel quick
  As an arrow went quivering by.

"Two and three, they came thicker, like horrible hail;
  Father groaned and looked white as a sheet,
When Carlo stretched out with a pitiful whine,
  And died in the road at our feet.

"But, grandmother, something we saw not at all
  Turned the darts off from father and me,
Just as if we were charmed."—Then grave Reuben spoke:
  "The child tells you truly," said he.

Then touched with his hand, powder-blackened and
    grim,
The great Bible that lay on the chair:
"Not a Pequod among them can feather a shaft
    But is turned by a good woman's prayer."

THE UNBIDDEN GUEST.

YOU would never guess, if you tried a year,
    Who came, an unbidden guest,
To the stylish wedding within the church,
    In a bridal garment dressed.

   *   *   *   *

Like a garden pathway the long aisle ran,
    'Twixt masses of shade and bloom,
Whilst the sunlight stole from the windows gay
    New tinting for robe and plume.

Society whispered in well-bred tones,
    And looked, as they came apace,
At each bidden guest.
                  Now a dowager
    In jewels and old point lace,
And robing of lavender (solemn hue
    That hints at the purple mist
Of the border province 'twixt youth and age
    By the sunset shadows kissed).

Now a banker, grave in his speckless suit,
    With satisfied, Dives air;
Now a maiden sweet as a drifted bloom;
    Now a matron young and fair.
All these, in their turn, trod the shadowed aisle,
    Led by courteous ushers bland,
And with silken rustle soon grouped themselves
    In the pews on either hand.

Still the echoing organ thrilled the air
    Through the arches far and wide;
Eager faces turned to the dusky door
    To watch for the coming bride,
When it opened,—shut,—then I saw her float
    Just within—the unbidden one—
With a silver star on her robe ashine
    Out of wondrous tissue spun.

Others saw her not. She was lowly born,
    Her home was upon the moor,
But the stars above, or an infant's breath,
    Were not, than her life, more pure.
Yet she seemed abashed, and she shrank away,
    Home-sick, an unwelcome guest,
Finding out, in truth, that Society
    On her wider life sore pressed.

Just before the bride and her maids came in,
    By a friendly zephyr fanned,
She came hither too, down the fragrant aisle,
    Never touching usher's hand;

For the royal sunshine uplifted her,
  And gave her a shining crown
Quite above them all.
            "Tell her name?" you ask:
  'Twas a star-eyed thistle-down!

GROWLER GRIM'S DREAM.

"WHY should I be so thankful, pray?"
  Grim Growler, reading, roughly spake.
"I've had my own hard row to hoe—
  My way all through the world to make;
I've earned the comforts that I own,
  I've rubbed my lot to make it bright;
I've toiled, as any man may do,
  And hold my place to-day of right."

Thanksgiving Eve! yet thankless thoughts
  Came trooping through old Growler's brain,
As he sat sipping crusty port
  And counting up his worldly gain.
Upon the printed page, laid down,
  Some words, it seemed, had caught his eye
Of thanks that were the morrow's due
  For blessings sent us from on high.

But when the twilight dusky grew,
  And leaping firelight flickered faint,
Beside his hearthstone something stood—
  A Presence, white robed like a saint;

Which, pointing to the ruddy gray
    Of failing fire, by current stirred,
Spake low and soft, and strangely sweet;
    "O mortal, thou hast greatly erred.

"Who keeps that wondrous metronome
    Of beating heart without thy care?
Who keeps the body safe in sleep,
    And wakes it to the morning fair?
You carved your lot? you asked for work?
    For capital your hands were all?
Who kept that right arm strong and sound?
    Who bade the rich man heed your call?

"Behold!" The rosy ashes stirred—
    A country-boy stood sad and shy
Before the mighty merchant-prince,
    With restless hands and drooping eye.
The while, until he turned, approved,
    A white-winged angel waited there,
Though neither boy nor master knew
    The fair shape of a mother's prayer.

Again the drifting ashes shone:
    "There go your ships safe to the land;
See you, above the tallest mast,
    The guidance of a shining hand?
You make your boast no missing ship
    Was ever marked from off your list:
Who gave the wild wind to your hand
    From out that mighty hollow fist?

"Look thou! Upon a couch of pain
    A baby weak and helpless lies;
Can you give back the rosy life
    That seems just nearing paradise?
Behold! Two angels bear the child
    Just near enough for God to kiss,
Then give it back to mother-arms
    To keep a while. Could you do this?

"When sore temptation trod the verge,
    And you came very near to fall,
Yet bounded back, you thought, O man,
    Your staunch resolve had done it all.
See! Yonder in the farm-house small,
    From which goes up a quiv'ring cry,
A gray-haired man lifts up his hands:
    'Thou, Lord, canst keep the boy—not I.'

"Oh, Growler Grim, walk softly now,
    Draw nearer with unshodden feet,
Lest step of thine may never fall
    Along that golden Upper Street!
Give back to Him His gifts to thee
    Through these, His poor, lest haply He,
In that bright harvesting to come,
    Alas! may not remember thee!"

*   *   *   *

When Growler Grim, out in the night,
    Sought humble homes of want and care,
With softened speech and open purse,
    How all the working-folks did stare!

For close beside his falling feet
  A shining footstep followed too,
And some saw gleaming wings anear,
  They softly said. Perhaps 'twas true.

IS IT WISE?

THE ring on my pretty friend's finger
  Is troth-plight, you say. Is it true?
All the upreaching dreams softly vanished,
  Because—bonny eyes are so blue?

Leaving starlight that bid her look upward,
  For glow-worm that lies at her feet,
Because—the thick locks are so golden;
  Because—the soft smile is so sweet.

Left the bridge to be trusted for ever,
  A stay for the foot evermore,
For the wearisome ford in the valley,
  Growing steep on the hitherward shore?—

Has she turned from the rock's steady shadow,
  Where trust would be safety alway,
To the gay little tent by the roadside
  A zephyr might shiver away?—

From the marble by skill fitly graven,
  With thought through its carving ashine,
To the image of clay gayly gilded,
  And painted with coloring fine?

Shall the vine, reaching upward no longer,
   To the plane of the oak never rise,
Catching now by the blossoming bramble?
   Is it true? Being true, is it wise?

I whisper no word of such musing,
   I say pretty words of the ring,
Hoping Love hath some infinite wisdom
   To answer my heart's questioning.

THE MIDNIGHT GUEST.

"IT is better so." 'Twas a woman's moan,
   Full of stifled tears. Where the lamplight shone
Through a vine-clad window, its ruddy glare
Made a lane of light in the sweet dark air,
For the rose that laughed in the sun all day
Dewy-laden hung in the yellow ray,
Where the tall white lilies shone out like stars,
And the very gate seemed of golden bars.

Weary, weak, and wan, like a hopeless shade,
Starting oft, as though of the winds afraid,
Like a spectre born of the solemn Night,
A woman stood in the lane of light.
Her unfastened hair in the dew-fall shone,
And her face was set like a face of stone,
As she muttered o'er, turning still to go,
"It is better, darling—yes, better so."

Then out into shadow and darkness fled,
While the summer night soft and silent sped,
Till the lamps were out, and the late moonlight
Came to midnight mass in his stole of white,
Bidding shadows kneel and their sins confess,
Laying on white hands like a priest to bless,
Touching light the dew on the shining spray
Of the censers swung by the lily's sway.

From the tree-top down came the silver glow,
Till it found a blotch on the summer snow—
Found a human life, hither brought to wait
For the hap and chance of a rich man's gate.
What remembered wrongs, what foreboding woe
From a cruel world, made it " better so,"
That a lonely waif in its wrappings stirred
With a sadder cry than a home-sick bird?—

Till the childless man from his slumber woke
As the baby's cry through the silence broke.
Ere the slippered feet and the lamp alight
Through the doorway came to the haunted night,
Came a rushing shape—sounded sweet and low
Little senseless words such as mothers know,
As the baby crept to its mother's breast,
While she murmured softly, "Nay, this is best."

As the oaken doorway was opened wide,
Eager faces questioned on either side,
But the sweet dark air of the night was still
As the swift feet sped o'er the dewy hill,

And the kindly heart never knew at all
How the air was stirred by the feeble call—
Never knew how near, in its robe of white,
A childish presence had crept that night.

THEN AND NOW.

1800.

SWAYING to and fro, see the reapers go,
  In the shine of the summer weather,
And they stop to hear if a lark sings clear,
  Or they laugh as they jest together.

An unhasting hand girdles sheaf with band,
  Slowly gathers the garnered treasure,
While the farm-horse waits by the open gates
  The slow time of the farmer's pleasure.

When the corn is bound, and there comes the sound
  Of the crows in the stubble calling,
Through the wide barn-door gleams the burdened floor,
  Sounds the cadence of swift flail falling.

Slowly jogging still over vale and hill,
  Golden grist to the mill is carried,
And the farmer waits, asking millers' rates,
  And the news of folks dead or married.

When the sacks of snow into biscuits blow,
    There is time for their rising given;
For the mystic spell modern grocers sell
    Was unknown in the days of leaven.

1878.

Quick work, sir! That biscuit, as light as a feather,
    Was only a wheat-ear five minutes ago! *
A match against time worth any man's watching,
    From golden wheat growing to edible snow.

'Twas fair, sir, to see, in the beautiful morning,
    The grain bow itself to a mastering will;
Watch the wheels of the reaper go over the stubble;
    Hear the swish of the knife in the summer air still.

Quick hands on the line caught the new-fallen treasure,
    Swiftly bore it away to the thresher's sure stroke,
Till each little grain shook itself, full of wonder
    At the pitiful loss of its golden-hued cloak.

Then away to the mill and the miller in waiting
    The horse seemed to fly with his load on his back;
His hoof-beats were taps on the bridge underneath him,
    The hand on the bridle no moment felt slack.

A whir of the mill; less than two minutes counted;
    Back again like the wind to the wide kitchen-door,

---

* The feat of a Carrollton (Mo.) farmer's family.

Where matron and maiden with deft fingers moulded,
  And swift the white heaps to the hot oven bore.

A kiss of the fire and the story is ended—
  Yes, less than five minutes from wheat-ear to bread.
So grow modern miracles; out of Time's sowing
  They spring into bloom 'neath a century's tread.

FORGIVE HER? NO, NEVER!

WELL, dominie, thank you for comin'—
  They told you, I s'pose, I was wild
When I found that a store-keepin' feller
  Had just run away with my child,
My baby, my motherless Nancy—
  She's a baby, you see, to me now—
And to think she would cheat her old father!
  "When was it?" you ask me, "and how?"

Well, 'long about hayin' she told me,
  Her apron half over her cheek,
That a lad from the town came a-courtin'.
  "Might she see him?" I tried not to speak,
But I couldn't keep still, an' I told her
  I'd shoot him as quick as a hound
If he ever come near her to court her
  When me and my gun was around.

She looked kind o' pitiful at me;
  "Oh, father, I've promised," she said,
And left me. Along through the orchard
  I saw the bent-down yaller head;
I saw her go wanderin' further;
  I knew well enough where she went,
For her mother lies buried off yonder,
  The way that her footsteps was bent.
An' she come when the dew was a-fallin'
  Apast me, with never a word;
But out at her own little window
  A pitiful sobbin' I heard.

    *   *   *   *   *

Well, after that, all through the summer,
  She seemed kind o' solemn and shy;
She said nothin' more of her lover,
  And nothin' about him said I.
Last night, when the milkin' was over,
  An' I sat by the stoop all alone,
Little Nancy came softly beside me,
  And took my old hand in her own.

Her face was as red as the roses,
  I know now she tried to confess
That her mind was made up to the weddin',
  But she hadn't the courage, I guess.

Well, sir, when I called in the mornin'
  No sleepy "Yes, father," I heard;
I opened the door of her chamber,
  And pillow and blanket wa'n't stirred.

All her poor little duds she had taken —
  There wa'n't such a wonderful sight—
And a shabby and faded old pictur'
  Of me, and her mother in white.

She left me this scrap of a paper;
  She's married by this time, you see.
You married her? Well, sir, how dare you
  Come over here talkin' to me?
Forgive her? No, never! no, never!
  She wants me to bless her? The jade!
She is waitin' out yonder? No matter,
  She must lie in the bed she has made.

I'll never, no, never forgive her!
  Who's comin'? Oh, Nancy, my child!
Ah me, she is like her dead mother!
    *   *   *   *   *
  Well, parson, we've got reconciled.

A LITTLE WHILE.

WHAT if the days are dreary?
  What if the desert glows
Beneath life's bitter sun-beat?
  What if the wild wind blows
Out of the North-Land stormy?
  What if Earth wears no smile?
A gate will open outward
  In such a little while!

If safely up to fourscore,
 We climb life's day-built stair,
How looks the way gone over,
 Still hand in hand with care?
Ah! life and all its doings
 Will seem but briefest text
To an unwritten sermon,
 This world so crowds the next.

What if we lack red roses,
 And laughter, and sweet song?
No matter, we are ending
 A journey never long.
How all the blooms of heaven
 Shall open to His smile,
We know not, but we shall know
 In such a little while.

What if the sweet child-voices
 No more may kiss your ear?
What if your hands are empty,
 Despoiled of jewels dear?
Let this sweet consolation
 Your daily grief beguile:
Betwixt good-bye and greeting
 Is such a little while.

Like ballast from an air-ship
 Our days drop out of sight,
So we may go up higher,
 Where seeming wrong shows right,

So, when we grow aweary
  Of pain, and loss and guile,
He whispers very softly,
  'Tis such a little while!

GRANDMOTHER'S LOVE-LETTER.

UP, up in the sunshiny garret,
  Where grandma's old treasures abide,
I can fancy her presence is near me—
  And creep, as of yore, to her side;
So, shutting my eyes, I recall her—
  The kindly old face in the cap,
The arm gently creeping about me
  As I hid childish woe in her lap.

The herbs that she long ago gathered,
  The fire-dogs ashine in the sun,
The spinning-wheel idle for ever,
  The blankets whose threads she had spun,—
Seem speaking, though silent around me
  These links of a life that I miss,
And the casket bequeathed with a blessing
  I touch with a reverent kiss.

As I open the time-yellowed packet,
  Writ "George to Amelia" without,
With a ribbon (that's made restitution
  Of sky-stolen blue) tied about,

GRANDMOTHER'S LOVE-LETTER.

I wonder if olden-time lovers
   Had tender and sweet things to say—
To think that this same "George" was grandpa,
   Not gouty, nor halting, nor gray!

"My darling Amelia"—that's grandma;
   Just fancy the blessed old dear
Being young and the belle of the village,
   In a bonnet and mantle so queer!—
"My darling Amelia,
                     Without you
   I find the days weary and long;"
This sounds very like Charlie's letter.
   Do they all sing the very same song?

Oh, grandpa, to think of your writing
   Such terrible nonsense as this,
About "love in a cottage," to grandma,
   With such a big "B" to the "bliss"!
Oh, you promise,
                "Most lovely Amelia,
   The winds shall not roughen your cheek;"
But, grandpa, how then did it happen
   You let her bring wood for a week?

I read: "When I win you, my darling,
   I'll guard you and keep you from care."
Oh, grandpa, who cured all the bacon?
   Who washed out the place for the fair?
"Ever sleeping or waking, Amelia,
   I'll keep thee from harm evermore."

Well, it sounds very funny to read it
    When I've heard the dear grandfather snore!

Did it seem just as charming to grandma
    As Charlie's dear letters to me,
When he writes of devotion and worship,
    And "bliss" with a proper-sized "b"?
Will somebody, some time, be reading
    With wonder the words I hold dear?
Will Twenty look backward at Threescore,
    Pronouncing its love-record queer?

MY NAMESAKE.

AH! never you'll guess, little baby,
    How fair are the visions I weave—
How earnest the wishes I whisper,
    How loving the kisses I leave

On lids like a late-folded rose-leaf,
    On nestled cheek downy and warm,
On mouth with its small dream aquiver,
    On fingers and vague battling arm.

This kiss I lay softly and slowly,
    And weigh it down thus, with a prayer
That a God-given guerdon of blessing
    May go with the name* you shall bear—

    * "Ethel"—noble. [Sax. Obs.]

That you wear it more worthily, darling,
    Than I in my weakness have done—
That it bring you for ever no sorrow
    Till the new name of heaven be won.

And this, on the mouth soft and rosy,
    That God, from the fountain above,
Shall give thee the beautiful blessing
    Of tender and true human love.

And this, on the pink palm unclosing,
    That Great-Heart shall still hold thee fast,
Till, Slough, Hill, and Valley gone over,
    He shall bring thee to Beulah at last.

THE DRAGON-FLY'S QUEST.

"What a shrill little scream, pretty Laura!
    Has a dragon leaped up from the lake?
I hear but the 'swish' of the rushes
    As shoreward our journey we take."

"Yes, here he is! There he is! Yonder!
    Now close to the water, now high."
"What, the dragon?"—"Yes, no; see him coming,
    Such a terrible blue dragon-fly!"—

"What a dear little goose! May I tell you
    The old German apologue fair
Of the dragon-fly's search o'er the water
    For the kin he left wondering there?

"In the solemn green water-world lying
  Slept the larvæ in peace long ago,
Till the sun, through the golden wave calling,
  Wakened surely the dull life below—

"Until creatures, new formed, woke to gladness—
  Strange gladness, not full, nor complete;
For the ooze of the soil was about them,
  And clung like a clog to their feet.

"Very wise water-bugs whispered softly
  That, climbing up rush-ladders high,
One could come to a kingdom of flowers,
  A land underneath a blue sky.

"Nay, that wings all unfettered went yonder,
  That death meant the water-line fair,
Where grossness of earth-form departed,
  And the freed spirit soared into air.

"There were doubters, of course, to dispute it;
  'What hath been shall be evermore,'
They said, as they clung to the rushes
  Or slept on the wave-covered shore.

"But the dragon-fly, steadily going
  Up higher toward sunlight divine,
Bade his comrades good-by as he pledged them
  A vow with the lily-root wine:

"'When I glow in the light I am seeking,
  And the kiss of the sun thrills me through,

I will watch for you here by the rushes,
    To tell you, O friends, it is true.'

"And so, little Laura, he's looking,
    To call out of ways dark and drear
Some creature that gropes in the shadow,
    Into glory and light, crystal clear."

TREE-TOP TROUBLE.

DO you think, little sorrowful lady,
    That no one has trouble but you?
When you wish to "be gay as a robin,"
    Remember, we robins get blue.

Aren't there bloodthirsty cats to appall us
    With fearful and terrible stare?
So a mother-bird never is happy,
    Nor free from solicitous care.

Why, the mischievous boys of the village
    I think will unsettle my brain,
When they threaten to torture and pillage,
    Regardless of protest or pain,

And then, Mr. Robin is careless—
    He don't stay at home as he should;
And if I reproach him he whistles,
    And flies to his club in the wood.

The nest, though I love it so dearly,
  Holds trouble and turmoil and sin,
For Jack, greedy bird! is the strongest,
  And grasps the supply I bring in,

While poor little Dick, thin and hungry,
  Feels slighted because he is small,
And Scrawney is always protesting
  I give him no dinner at all.

There was Sweetie, who fell in the fountain,
  Out looking for me from the nest;
It seems to me always that Sweetie
  Was dearest and brightest and best.

So you see, little sorrowful lady,
  That even the birds of the air
Cannot fly from the ills that beset them,
  Nor flutter through life without care.

There is sorrow for women, for robins—
  In tree-top and wide dwelling too—
But I know of a country that's better
  To seek in the autumn—do you?

THE ROSE OF THE RING.

"WELL, Nelly, I'm sorry a'most, after all,
    That I took you to see the big show:
A circus is not very much to my taste,
  But I knew how you wanted to go.

"I feel kind o' sober to think all the while
  That the chaps ridin' round with a grin
Would be glad to get out of that life if they could;
  But they wouldn't know where to begin.

"The 'Rose of the Ring' looked so happy, you say,
  As she rode the black horse on the ground;
And she had on a bracelet and ear-rings that shone,
  Velvet bodice and skirt spangled round?

"'An' her hair hangin' down in a tangle of curls
  Wasn't finer than yours?' No, indeed!
When she smiled as the people applauded her skill,
  Ridin' round at the top of her speed,

"You felt as if tendin' the work of the farm
  Was *so* dreary and hopeless and slow;
Washing dishes, and churning, and mending old coats
  Seemed so stupid and doleful, I know.

"But if you'd been over the dressin'-room side,
  And heard what I did, standin' there,
Where her brute of a husband stood waitin' for her;
  How he clutched at her long curly hair;

"How he stamped and he swore with a terrible cry,
  As he flung her, poor girl! to the ground,
Because, being weary, she slipped off her horse
  When she should have leaped up at a bound!

THE ROSE OF THE RING.

"You wouldn't thought then, as she whimpering stood,
   That her life was a happy one, dear;
Each spangle a-quiverin' over her breast
   Seemed to me but a pitiful tear.

"That's the way, Nelly dear, that the 'Rose of the Ring'
   Earns her bread. Would you change if you could?"
By the rough farmer's side, with her head on his breast,
   Little Nelly, his girlish wife, stood.

"Oh, John! I believe you see into my heart,
   For you know without speaking my thought;
And then you're so patient and tender and good!
   Never scolding me well, as you ought.

"I *was* thinking, dear, how dull home would seem;
   How I hated my old gray delaine,
And the milk-pail, and dishes, and ironing-board;
   But, John, I won't do so again.

"A heart such as yours, John, a temper so kind,
   Are far better than jewels to me;
And the spangles ashine on the glittering skirt
   Only tear-drops henceforth I shall see."

TIME'S TRIUMPH.

1859.

"MOTHER," said pretty May,
    Fresh graduate from school,
Looking about the homestead,
    Within its wide hall cool,
At oaken chair and sideboard,
    And tall clock on the stair,—
"Please listen, mother dearest:
    Would grandma, think you, care

"If those old things were banished
    To lumber-rooms away?
Grand things they were in her times,
    But look so queer to-day.
Look at the old blue china
    Displayed on wall and shelf,
As tho' we had no French ware
    To use instead of delf.

"That spinning-wheel looks horrid,
    Old-fashioned as the sun;
'Twas very well in old times,
    When ev'ry lady spun.
That spider-legged piano
    Is jangled so, you know;
Those candlesticks and fire-dogs
    Do mortify me so!"

1879.

"Oh, mother dear!" A matron
  Sedate was daughter May,
With merry childish trio
  Making a summer stay
Within the quiet homestead—
  Wiser and gentler grown
Since those far days of girlhood
  Had swiftly backward flown.

The "grandma," well remembered
  In household legends sweet,
Had found herself old-fashioned
  As years fell round her feet,
And so went up one morning
  To friends of bygone years,
To find one blessèd fashion
  That hides all pain and tears.

So now when children's voices
  Called "Grandma!" it was she
Who once was only "Mother"
  Who answered claimants three—
Half wond'ring at the echo,
  Half questioning if she
Had gone adown life's valley
  Past milestones sixty-three.

"Mother, I've such a favor
  To ask you, if I dare.

I'm furnishing my new home;
  I wonder, would you spare
That old Dutch clock up garret,
  And spinning-wheel, to me?
The fire-dogs—do you use them?
  And candlesticks? You see

"I can buy new ones, gorgeous,
  But these are dearer far;
And that old delf—I'd like it,
  In spite of nick and mar.
I won't ask for the sideboard,
  For that I know you care,
But there's the old piano—
  Why, mother, how you stare!"

THE DAFFODILS NEVER FORGET.

I THOUGHT some petitions of mine
  Were unanswered as days hurried by,
And so I went groping in mist,
  When I should have looked up to the sky;

Until, looking still at the earth
  As I sat in the old cottage-door,
'Mid dreams of the shadowy feet
  That should enter that threshold no more;

I saw, by the foot-trodden stone,
  Through the crevices threading the mould,

Pale malachite shafts bearing up
   Caskets brimming with daffodil gold.

Ah! then I remembered it all:
   It was there in November I laid
Some titles to sunshine away—
   Folded promises sure to be paid;

And then had forgotten them all,
   Since crystalline·snow-flowers white
Had hid the brown earth underneath,
   'Twixt darkness and dawning, one night—

Forgot to look down by the door
   When the blue-birds were carolling clear—
Forgot when the robins came nigh,
   Looking over the nests of last year.

But all the time, softly and sure,
   The sunshine befriended the spot,
And though I forgot they were there,
   The daffodils never forgot.

And thus it seems helpful to know,
   When our eyelids with weeping are wet,
And weary with waiting the while,
   God and daffodils never forget.

A LOVER'S STRATAGEM.

STILL love me, little sweetheart,
   Until arbutus pale
Above the snow shall blossom,
   And brighten all the vale.

Arbutus-bloom is fading;
   Oh promise, sweetheart, still
To love me till the blowing
   Of golden daffodil.

Alas! my little sweetheart,
   The daffodils are dead;
Wilt love me till the roses
   Unfold their robes of red?

Ah! roses die so quickly,
   All smothered with perfume;
Don't quite forsake me, darling,
   Until the dahlias bloom.

Nay, one more promise, sweetheart:
   Since dahlias have gone by,
Keep faith till everlastings
   Shall bloom and fade and die.

Thus wisely sped my wooing
   Through blossom-epochs fair,
And this is why I treasure
   This fadeless flower with care.

IN DANGER.*

AFRAID? When I stood up yonder
    On the bow of a boat ashore,
With a rent in her black hull riven,
    Through which flood and death might pour?

'Mid the sound of the midnight echo,
    "Climb ashore! for the boat may sink!"
Looking up at the dark, high mountain,
    At the river as black as ink?

Yes, I was afraid—of the water,
    That glimmered so dark and cold;
Afraid of the coming struggle
    That the midnight call foretold;

Afraid of the cruel sharpness
    Of rocks under naked feet;
Afraid of the newsboy's story
    To sound in the city street;

Afraid that the souls belovèd
    Should garner no good-bye kiss,
Or find no grave grass-covered—
    Afraid? Yes, afraid of this.

* On board the Catskill boat Walter Brett, which, with a sleeping pilot, ran on the rocks at midnight, September 28th. The sharp rocks or the deep water presented the only alternatives at first. Happily, another boat, which had been watching the erratic course of the Brett, soon came to the rescue.

But oh! in that solemn midnight,
   To find that the anchor cast
In the blood-bought promise held me
   To the blessed life-line fast!—

That I had no swift accounting
   To do with a whirling brain,
Only kiss the hand outreaching,
   The palm with its crimson stain,

That in years agone had blest me,
   And covered my load of sin,
Which held—not a rod to fright me—
   But a beacon to light me in.

HILL AND SHORE.

OH the hills! the hills! I am sick for the hills,
   With their warm brown sides so bare,
Their circling arms, and their steady feet
   On the shadows slumbering there;

With their reverent hands to the sky upraised
   As they pray on their carpets green,
Seeking evermore what the angels see
   In the Land still to us unseen.

A while this surge of the solemn sea,
   And the moan of its deep unrest,
And then I turn like a home-sick child,
   Happy hills! to your riven breast.

Some gleams of light from the sunset gate,
   Bright over the purple sea—
Some charges made on the battered coast
   By its white-horse cavalry—

Some sleepy dreams by its lapping waves—
   Some trysts with the stars and sun,—
And then, old friends, take me home again,
   With my heart from you still unwon.

O grand old hills! that my eye can trust
   With your changeless outline kept
Since the fiat "Light!" o'er the new world thrilled,
   And the sun to its music stepped.

I am glad to think in your keeping sure
   I shall rest after work is past,
And the warm brown arms of the patient mould
   Shall be softly round me cast,

Where the friends I love, when a daisy blooms
   Above me, its face shall kiss;
O grasping arms of the sliding sea!
   Can your blue waves promise this?

A QUESTION.

MUST we always keep Thanksgiving
   When the cold November rain
Blurs the loving faces watching
   For us through the window-pane,

A QUESTION.

All because our Pilgrim Fathers,
   One November long ago,
In the wilderness were thankful,
   Spite of winter wind and snow.

Can't we start anew to keep it,
   Loving them the while as well,
When the glory of October
   Burns on mountain-tops and dell—

When "the baby," lightly hooded,
   Safely from its home may come—
The busy man fear no delaying,
   Rails snow-fettered, wire-speech dumb;

And the baby's fragile mother
   Need not fear the autumn's frown,
Or grandmamma risk retribution
   Donning cap and silken gown—

When the homestead-door may open
   To the sunshine pure and sweet,
And the dropping gold of maples
   Stir beneath the welcome feet—

Whilst the hillsides wear their greenness,
   And along the sunset sky
Serried ranks of corn-stacks, banded,
   Still their rustling pennons fly.

Pumpkin-pies might glimmer golden
   Wreathed with blossoms brave and gay;

Queenly dahlias to the turkey
　　Bow in their own royal way.

Wreath and bough, of autumn crimson,
　　Gleam on wall and mirror quaint,
And about the picture cherished
　　Of the vanished household saint.

Ah! with all respect to Pilgrims,
　　Comes the question once again :
Must we keep Thanksgiving always
　　Through November's sullen reign?

THE FARMER'S WIFE.

WHEN there echoes the roll-call of honor
　　Amid the white ranks of the blest,
And over the heads bowed in answer
　　The crown of well-doing shall rest,

I seem to see, brightest among them,
　　The farmer's wife faithful and true,
Her worn, weary hands folded idly,
　　Her wearisome duties all through.

The farmer is out in God's sunshine ;
　　Fellow-workman with him is his God ;
Sun and seed, frost and plough, work together,
　　And daisies smile up from the sod ;

But the cellar, the milk-room, the kitchen,
   To bake and to sweep and to sew,
From rising of sun to its setting,
   Is the round of her days, never new.

From the kitten that plays on the threshold,
   To the harvest-hands, hungry and brown,
Her thought must be ever unceasing,
   Her care for them never laid down.

O strong man, bring in from the meadow
   Kind words to the worker inside,
And remember the true, faithful helper
   May falter some time from your side.

Then your eyes will be opened in wonder
   That, blinded, you let her toil on,
Till the bride you once promised to cherish,
   The mother, the housewife, is gone.

Then the worn face at rest in the coffin
   Its pitiful story shall tell.
O busy man, stop in the furrow,
   If needs be, to think, Is it well?

OFF BARNEGAT.

SUNSET, athwart the winter sea,
　Kissed keel, and sail, and tall masts three
Of a schooner nearing Barnegat.
The captain's wife in the cabin sat,
With warm arms round her baby fair,
And cheek bent o'er its yellow hair.
Fearless alike of wind and sea,
She rocked and sang contentedly,
Or stooped the baby brow to kiss
And wondered idly if 'twould miss
Her clasp if aught should part them now,
Then kissed again from baby's brow
The thought, and sang the lullaby
That held her dream of harbor nigh.
The captain wiped his dimming glass
From mist, and said, "God bless the lass!"
The list'ning sailors lightly stepped
Or one by one to hear her crept,
As though, some way, the sweet air drew
Their better selves above the blue,
And home and God seemed strangely nigh
As still she sang "Sweet by and bye."

*　　　*　　　*　　　*

Ere midnight passed or morning broke,
Ere little child or mother woke,
Came crash and cry—came falling spar.
The Tolck was stranded on the bar!

Hoarse voices shouted; swinging low
Great sails, ice-mailed, flapped to and fro;
White faces showed when through the night
Shone rocket's flash and Coston-light,
And strong men shuddered as the sea
Broke o'er the stern relentlessly.

"Men, save yourselves!" the captain said;
"My place is here, alive or dead.
  Save wife and child!"
                    Strong helpers drew
Mother and child the stairway through—
Lashed to the mast with tender care
The captain's wife.
                Pale, calm, and fair,
She wrapped her child in scarf and shawl,
Then whispered to the first mate tall,
"Save her for me, Ben. I will bide
Through peril at the captain's side."

Across the sullen ocean's roar
Came voices nearer on the shore,
Till in the morning's early light
They saw, beyond the breakers white,
A score of men with helpful hands
Dragging in haste along the sands
Life-car and buoy, line and gun.
Up through the air the life-line spun,

And fell—six fathoms short!
                    Once more
It flew; it linked the ship to shore!
Along the rope, to strong rings tied,
The life-car gained the schooner's side;
The mate made ready for his care
The baby safe ashore to bear.
The mother's lips moaned out, "Good-bye!
You'll save her, Ben?"
                    A hoarse "Ay! ay!"
Through roar of surf and deep sea-moan
Came floating back to watcher lone.
Too cold her hands to fold in prayer,
Her eyes yet watched the canvas chair,
Up rising now, now lost to sight,
Till safely through the breakers white
It reached the welcome waiting shore.
Three ringing cheers the salt air bore,
And waiting arms the salvage fair
Took safely from the tall mate's care,
Whilst from the ship, like faintest sigh,
There echoed still "Sweet by and bye."

With dawning wild winds rougher grew;
No boat could live that white surf through.
The captain bid his men at last
Lash him as well against the mast,
So he might hold the figure frail
Better against the icy gale—

Wrapped his wide cloak to shield from harm
The fair head drooping on his arm,
And whispered softly,
                    "You and I
Will reach port soon!"
                    Her glazing eye
Turned shoreward first, then glanced aloft,
Whilst trembled still that echo soft,
Until, with head low on his breast,
The song came to an endless rest.
Thus morning found them, white and chill,
Beyond the touch of human ill,
Safe on the Frost-king's stalwart arm
From heartache sore or body's harm.

    *   *   *   *

Now, when dark winter's icy breath
Brings solemn tales of wreck and death,
Whilst watching through the midnight dark
For homeward step and lantern's spark,
In fishing-cabins old wives tell
Again the tale all know so well.
Just when the drift-wood fire burns low,
And loitering neighbors turn to go,
They stop and listen by the door
And hear, they say, though wild seas roar,
Clearly and softly, floating nigh,
That faith-song still,
                    "Sweet by and bye!"

REUNITED.

WATCHING, watching by the portal
    Of the city's golden street,
Still a childish angel lingered,
    Maidenly and strangely sweet.

All the bright ones swiftly passing
    Blessed her on their outward way,
As she whispered, "Is my mother
    Coming, angel fair, to-day?"

When the hosts who do His bidding
    Sped, their waiting harps to tune,
Each one met the patient query,
    "Is my mother coming soon?"

"I came on with Jesus early,
    Clinging to His piercèd hand;
Will she find me, coming later
    Up to Him and Glory-Land?

"It seems ages since I left her—
    Ages since she kissed my hair;
Can you tell me, kindly angels,
    Why does mother tarry there?"

When a silver shadow brightened
    Up from earth to gate of pearl,
Lo! a mother, angel-guided,
    Sought and found her little girl;

And when, up through the blessed city,
   Hand in hand, the twain drew near
To waiting ones, there sounded softly,
   O'er and over, "Mother's here!"

A BACHELOR'S BRIDE.

I WONDER where I missed you, dear,
   My wife that should have been,
And when I nearest stood to you,
   My little love, unseen?

Perhaps I passed you long ago,
   Yet never bird or bee,
With happy song or sombre drone,
   Betrayed the fact to me.

Perhaps across the ocean now
   You stare at foreign wonders,
Grow wise in Rome, or poetize
   Amid Chamounix' thunders.

Perhaps we may not meet at all,
   And so ask each for ever,
Why some unmated souls there are
   Who find love's answer never?

I'll write out those I best have known,
   With some I never knew,
And choose by lot, my wife to be,
   First—Margaret, fair friend and true.

Then Kate and Jo, and Sue and Rose;
  Now for some names unknown—
Anita, Eleanor, Fanchette,
  And Gretchen by the Rhone.

Ah! here comes Margie: "Little friend,
  I'm looking for my wife,
The woman I have missed somewhere,
  And so lived half a life."

See! now I draw the magic slip,
  And read it, "Gretchen!" Where
Has Margie gone? Why did she blush
  Up to her very forehead fair,

As though it had been her own name?
  Stop! "Gretchen" is her own
In accents of the "Faderland"—
  The same. I might have known

That fact at first. O childish friend!
  Have I been mad or blind,
That all at once I see the truth,
  And wake from dreams, to find

The dearest girl in all the world
  Treading life's walk with me?
Ah! after all these blinded years,
  Like him once healed I see.

AN OLD MAN.

"OLD man, old man, coming up the road!
   Run, girls! run fast to the school-house door!"
There they go, pell-mell, like a flock of sheep,
   As I plod along, weary, weak, footsore.
Do I look so old bearing thirty years?
   Have I then indeed such a terror grown
That the children scare at my near approach
   On this old highway, long ago well known?

Weak and wicked both; I deny it not—
   Old in sin I am since I walked this way,
But the years are few since I fled at night;
   Ah! the flitting seems but as yesterday,
When sore from the stripes that I had not earned
   That time (though I had many times before),
I flung myself in the moonlight pale
   Down, to lay my face on the garret-floor.

When the stolen steps of my mother came,
   And her little figure all clad in white
Like a blessed angel came drifting in
   Where a wreck I lay in the fair moonlight,
How she kissed the bruise on the swollen cheek,
   While her tears fell like bitter rain!
How the loyal wife with the mother strove!
   Well! the grave-sod covers her wrong and pain.

"Old man! Old man!" I will turn aside,
   I remember well that a quiet pool

AN OLD MAN.

Over yonder sleeps where the wooded slope
   Lays a smooth cheek down by its rim to cool.
I will look to see if this face of mine
   Shall the tale confirm that the children tell;
No silver tangles my unkempt beard,
   And my strong white teeth gnaw a crust full well.

Now I peer out over the mossy rock.
   See! a beggar's rags flutter first in view;
Then untended locks like a wild beast's mane,
   And the shoulders bent. Childish eyes see true!
For the added "naught" of a beggar's year
   Counts for ten, it seems, to the eyes that see
Through the morning light. Ah, the school is in,
- And the weary road stretches out for me.

Passing close again by the school-house door,
   Sounds a blessed word that beguiles the way,
As the teacher reads from the Holy Book
   All the sweet old tale of the lad astray—
Of the Father's watch, of the welcome kiss.
   He lifts his hat from his forehead bare,
And the dusty lips murmur, "If I came
   From the 'country far,' would the Father care?"

THE SNOW THAT LIES BETWEEN.

I KNOW autumn's beautiful slumber
   Is only a rest-giving sleep,
That trees only throw down their jewels
   For the Ethiop, Earth, safe to keep.

I know these cold winds of November
   Will blow till fair April sheds tears,
When, looping from harvest to sowing,
   Still stretches the vine of the years.

I know yonder knoll clad in stubble
   Will glow in its spring suit of green;
And yet, knowing all, I remember
   A winter's snow lies in between.

Will it cover some heartache or trial
   With crystalline glittering show?
Will it borrow some treasure I cherish
   To hide underneath the white snow?

So silent its white hand falls softly,
   Will it give me aught back when it lifts,
Or lie over some buried purpose,
   Some pitiful wide-gaping rifts?

Nay, rather I'll think that some blossom
   Is hidden till spring-time unseen,
And so, like a patient bird brooding,
   Dread not though the snow lies between.

SYMPATHY.

AH, wise man, who counsels us sagely,
   Strong woman, by sorrow untried,
Don't talk to the soul grown aweary,
   Or the body that smitten has cried,

Until the same chrism has touched you,
   Your lips tasted Marah as well,
Else words kindly spoken lack wisdom—
   Lack sympathy's comforting spell.

Business failure comes down on your neighbor;
   You call, and you're sorry, you say;
Your own gilded threshold untarnished,
   What know you of down-trodden clay?

Ailing Robin groans over his sickness;
   His duty of patience seems plain,
But all the while you must remember
   The fact that it isn't *your* pain.

Or the son of a widow goes seeking
   His fortune. You hear it with joy,
And strongly condemn her lone weeping;
   But, wise man, it wasn't *your* boy.

A daughter has married and vanished,
   A mother cries softly to miss
The song in the house and the footstep,
   The morning and night-given kiss;

You whisper old trite consolations,
    Submission to things that must be ;
It wasn't *your* trial, wise woman—
    It wasn't *your* daughter, you see !

Above a short grave softly sighing,
    A young mother weeps night and day ;
"It was only a baby," you whisper :
    It was hers—and was taken away !

AUNT ABBY'S WINGS.

"WELL, children"—the father spoke slowly,
    As one who has bad news to tell,
Looking round on the half-score of youngsters,
    And round at his helpmeet as well—

"It appears Uncle Abram left nothing ;
    He died in the West a poor man ;
Can we make a warm place for Aunt Abby?—
    Mother Ruth, do you think, dear, we can?"

Then the house-mother, shutting down softly
    Some housekeeper's doubts out of sight,
Giving up in her heart the big closet,
    The "spare room" draped newly in white,

Beating back all the questions she queried—
    If Abby would worry at noise ?
Was she nervous or full of queer notions ?
    Would she lecture and scold the two boys ?—

Still answered, "We'll welcome Aunt Abby;
   Won't we, children?" as brave as could be;
And Jotham said softly, "God bless her!
   I knew very well how 'twould be."

So she came with an October sunset·
   (And the stage) to the wide-open door—
A meek little form, clad in mourning,
   A waif from Death's desolate shore.

You never would guess that an angel
   Could come in a stage, without wings;
But the household of Jotham will tell you
   'Tis one of life's possible things.

When the fever came stealthily creeping,
   And touched, save herself, every one,
Did Abby need wings to proclaim her
   A blessing as bright as the sun?

Didn't *she* hold the mother's head drooping?
   Didn't *she* rock the baby to rest?
Didn't *she* kiss the boys ev'ry morning,
   And cuddle Kit up on her breast?

And when the sad season was over,
   And health came among them to stay,
When the circle at prayers rounded perfect,
   And Jotham could say, "Let *us* pray,"

Giving true hearty thanks for all mercies
   By which the dark hours had been blest,
Ruth whispered "Amen" while he counted
   As the chiefest and dearest their guest.

GOING TO SLEEP.

STEPPING straight off the shore
   Of a twilight frolic gay
Into the arms of Sleep—
   That is the baby's way.
Down, till the tender mouth
   Quivers with baby-dreams,
And the silver dew of sleep
   On the nestled forehead gleams.

Making good fight a while,
   Rubbing with school-boy fist
His eyes, till lights about
   Shimmer in rings of mist,
With many a dreaming start
   Of playground's scare or leap,
Till the rough red hands lie still—
   So Freddie goes to sleep.

Nellie, with half-shut eyes,
   Drifts onward dreamily
Through the happy border-land
   Of a moonlight reverie,
Until, like a folded rose,
   Or lily of the lake,
Sleep shuts her senses up
   Till a new dawn awake.

Protesting stoutly still
   Against Sleep's mastery,

The busy man lies down
  To think.
          His reverie
Is strongly vocal soon,
  The face, off guard, grows sad,
Spite of the trumpet tune.

And grandma, dear old soul!
  Asleep in easy-chair,
Denies it when the lads
  Laugh at her stony stare,
Her dear old nodding head,
  And hands that will unlock,
Till knitting-needles fall
  From the unfinished sock.

THE BURIED SHIP.

THE wild winter wind and the restless wave
  Have upraised a wreck from its ocean grave.
Down at Aquebogue fishers used to show
Where the Mars went down fifty years ago.
'Twas a trading brig from a tropic shore
That sank from sight to the ocean floor,
By the sexton, sand, buried well and deep
Till the winter storm called her up from sleep.

Like a ghost she came. Seaward-looking eyes
Saw an outline new on the sea and skies;
Watching fisher-folks, half afraid, drew near,
Till they saw her decks through the water clear.

Then the wise old salts by the firesides said,
With many a shake of each whitened head,
They remembered well that October blow
And the sinking wreck fifty years ago.

Old ship! awaked from your solemn sleep
On the sifted sand of the silent deep,
Do you come for news from the nigh mainland
That northward crescents yon strip of sand?
Have you come to watch with a jealous eye
How the wingless steamship bustles by?
Have you heard the call of the cable's thrill
As it pulsed some echo of human will?

Have the parted links of a riven chain
Jangled down to tell of a great wrong slain?
Have the ruddy drops of a soldier's blood
Never brought war-news on the ebbing flood,
Nor wave astray from the Gulf Stream's tide
Told of yellow gold where the sunsets hide—
Never home-sick heart 'neath a miner's tent
From the far Sierras a cloud-kiss sent?

Do you miss the souls into harbor passed
Since the sunbeams gilded your gallant mast?
Through the rapid flight of the buried years
Heard you never of stranded hopes and fears?
So, finding the world would not come to thee,
Hast thou come, old ship, for thyself to see,
Like a sleeper sound, who has lain too long,
Wakened up at last by a fisher's song?

BABY-LOVE.

HARK! "Nobody cares for us old folks."
   The wind's turning eastward, I know,
Else dear little Grandmother Berry
   Would never be murmuring so,
Or put a small end of her cap-string
   Right into a gathering tear,
Or choke out a tremulous answer,
   "There's nothing the matter, my dear."

She's feeling quite pitiful somehow,
   Neglected and lonesome, dear heart!
Maybe we forget years are wedging
   The young and the old folks apart.
Perhaps in this busy existence
   We do not remember to say
The small loving words in the household,
   To brighten for some one the day.

But see! there is wee baby-lassie
   Stretching out eager arms with a cry,
And straightway, 'mid loving caresses,
   That cap-string comes out of the eye;
The wind shifts due west in a hurry
   When "Bessie loves dan-ma" is said,
And I fancy Love shines like a glory
   Around Bessie's close-nestled head.

O babies! with fingers like rose-leaves
   To touch wounded spirits so near,

When the Master so long ago blessed you
   He gave you a mission, 'tis clear;
For babies love old folks—God bless them !—
   They miss not the golden locks gone;
They see not the eventide shadow
   Eclipsing Life's roseate dawn.

Nay, clearer of vision, it may be,
   Since nearer than we to the sky,
They see the ripe heart's tender treasure,
   And pass youth and beauty both by.
So, grandma, "your case is not proven."
   That babies love old folks is plain;
And Bessie shall help me to prove it
   If I hear any mourning again.

THE BABY'S COMING.

NOW for a summer sojourn sweet,
   My cares all left behind me,
My law-books left to gather dust,
   While clients cannot find me.
The bed and board are promising—
   Nay, better still, are proving
In strict accord with contract made
   Before my summer moving.

Alas! to-day I heard them say
   What filled my heart with sorrow:

"The baby's coming very soon;
  And may be here to-morrow."
I didn't know a baby lived
  Within a furlong here;
Not that I sanction Herod's plan,
  But then—they cry. Oh dear!

I know there will be silver spoons
  That smell of paregoric,
I know there will be wails by day,
  And nights most melancholic.
The doors must all be shut, no doubt,
  If "baby" dear should sneeze;
The "baby's" carriage in the hall
  Must graze the boarders' knees.

Where did I leave off journal-leaves?
  Ah, here, "the baby" dreading.
Such queer events since then have come
  Close on each other treading!
The "baby"! Well, the baby came,
  Is here to-day, God bless her!
And I have learned to love it well—
  Would, if I dared, caress her.

* * * *

So I sat down at breakfast-time
  A little sulky maybe,
And then—the morning brighter grew
  With advent of—"the baby."
A lady fair, with starry eyes
  With summer sleep yet dewy,

Was introduced. "O summer guest!
    This is our baby, Louie."

I look back on my journal now
    To scratch out what is written
Of fear and dread. I nothing fear
    From "baby" now—except the mitten.
I am not sure, I dare not ask,
    Lest she might scorn me, maybe,
If I should offer heart and hand
    Most humbly to "the baby."

VERY EARLY.

VERY early in the morning
    Of the new week's dawning day,
Like one blessèd, past the angels
    Baby darling stole away.

Was there ever softer summons,
    Sweeter time on earth, than this,
For a creature surely ransomed
    To receive the heavenly kiss?

True, we saw no shining angels
    When their broad wings, wide and white,
Swept the cradle, cold and empty,
    Just as dawn bloomed out of night—

Heard no clear angelic voices,
    Such as thrilled on Mary's ear:

"Ye seek the Lord? Lo! He is risen!
Ye seek the Lord? He is not here."

But through cloud-encompassed glory
   Piercèd hands, that once were laid
On childish heads, reached down to take him,
   Safely, softly, unafraid.

Wiser now than Eastern Magi
   'Neath the strange Judean star,
Is the creature newly entered
   In beyond the crystal bar—

Safer than the nested robin
   Hovered 'neath its mother's breast;
Nearer in its tender silence
   Than the folded darling blest.

Ah! I hear an angel whisper,
   "Nay, not here for Baby seek;
He, like Jesu, vanished early
   In the dawning of the week."

THE LETTERS THAT COME NOT.

NAY, Flossie, my fair little maiden,
   Don't frown as the postman goes by,
Nor twist up your bit of a kerchief
   To wipe a small tear from your eye.

THE LETTERS THAT COME NOT.

"No letter? And you're disappointed,
   A little bit (whisper it) cross,
Because you must wait till to-morrow
   To read the old story, 'Dear Floss'?"

Ah! sweetheart, have patience yet longer;
   'Twill come by and by, safe and sure,
Though the waiting for love or a lover
   Grows hard for the young to endure.

But we, who live nearer Life's shadows,
   Have learned that no present "to-day"
Glows ever so fair as that "morrow"
   That peers over nightfall alway.

Besides, in the days of our sojourn
   Have come, in their white paper cloaks,
Through the post, very sorrowful stories—
   Sad words that have scarred us like strokes.

And now, when there cometh no tidings,
   We learn to be patient and wait,
Right glad for the missive that comes not,
   As well as for these at the gate—

Right glad that the bundle of letters
   Held tight in the messenger's hand,
For us held no goblin to frighten,
   Nor tale of a broken home-band—

No thorn of distrust with its poison,
   No arrow to smite into pain,

No reproach for shortcomings or failure,
  No whisper of struggle or stain.

So out of to-day's disappointment,
  Dear Flossie, we'll gather no rue;
The letters that don't come are painless;
  Are we sure of the letters that do?

THE VOICE OF THE CHILDREN'S BELL.

A BELL was bought for the new church-tower;
  It had godly girth and a mighty tongue;
Strong and skilful hands raised it carefully
  Till above, in the belfry, it safely swung.

Then the earnest ones who had built the church
  Wandered out afar, that they there might hear
The resounding notes of the great new bell
  Echoed far and wide, vibrant, sweet, and clear.

Alas! when the stroke on the clear air smote
  But a little chime from the belfry rang,
Instead of the echoing thunder-tone
  They had waited for when the bell should clang.

There was question sharp, there was wonder wide,
  There was new adjustment to and fro,
But still the bell sounded far away,
  And its voice still echoed small and low.

Is it only a dreamer's fancy, then,
  That I call to mind, 'twas the children gave
To the church its bell? that the name it bears
  Is written over a little grave?

Does the brazen mass keep a loyal heart
  In remembrance still of a childish saint,
And is that the reason evermore
  Why the tones evoked echo far and faint?

Only idle fancy, I know, all this,
  And yet when I hear the pathetic peal,
I wonder still if the children's bell
  Is not stamped in truth with the children's seal.

HUM-BIRD AND BUMBLE.

WEE Bobbie, and Nettie, and Willie,
  Come here, on the grass by my knee,
Till I tell you about a great battle
  It fell to my fortune to see.

Busy Bumble-bee found a sweet lily
  With rosy silk curtains inside,
And crept for a nap in its hollow,
  Intending till morn to abide.

How he snored! Yes, I heard him so loudly!
  I laughed at his perfect content,

While the beautiful blossom drooped over,
    And the sturdy green lily-stem bent.

Like a jewel with wings fluttered Hum-bird—
    Fair Hum-bird, sweet child of the air—
Seeking eagerly food from the lily,
    Unconscious that Bumble was there.

With wings blurred by rapid vibration,
    With a ruby ablaze on her breast,
Her tongue like a fairy tape-measure,
    Unrolled, for its sweet honey-quest,

Came the bird to the lily-tent swiftly;
    Old Bumble woke cross as could be,
As he backed himself out of his quarters,
    And turned his queer eyes round to see.

And he growled and he hummed and he threatened,
    While Hum-bird said, plain as could be,
"Hurry out, right away, from my lily!"—
    "*Your* lily!" growled Bumble; "we'll see."

Then they fought with a will. Little Hum-bird
    Struck wildly with beak, claw, and wing,
Till old Bumble, in terrible temper,
    Pierced the beautiful breast with his sting.

There was one little squeak as it ended,
    And poor little Hum-bird lay dead;
So I buried her softly in rose-leaves,
    And laid a bud under her head.

How I smote Bumble-bee with my kerchief,
And tore up the lily he stole!
But was glad, all the while, to remember
Wee Hum-bird had never a soul.

BABY IS KING.

A ROSE-CURTAINED cradle,
    Where, nestled within
Soft cambric and flannel,
    Lie pounds seventeen,
Is the throne of a tyrant;
    That pink little thing
Is an autocrat august,
    For Baby is king.

Good, solemn grandfather
    Dares hardly to speak
Or walk, lest the sleeper
    Should hear his boots creak;
Grandma is a martyr
    In habits and cap,
Which the monarch unsettles
    As well as her nap.

Papa, wise and mighty,
    Just home from the House,
Grows meek on the threshold,
    And moves like a mouse

To stare at the bundle;
   Then onward he goes,
Like an elephant trying
   To walk on his toes.

The queen of the ballroom
   Throws loyally down
Before him the roses
   She wore in her crown,
And sings little love-songs
   Of how she loves best
The fair baby blossom
   She rocks on her breast.

Good aunties and cousins
   Before him bow low,
Though he rumples the ringlets,
   Twists collar and bow;
He bids the nurse walk
   With His Majesty's self,
And cries when she stops,
   Like a merciless elf.

He flings right and left
   His saucy fat fist,
And then the next moment
   Expects to be kissed.
He demands people's watches
   To batter about,
And meets a refusal
   With struggle and shout.

Then, failing to conquer,
    With passionate cry
He quivers his lips,
    Keeps a tear in his eye,
And so wins in the battle,
    This wise little thing;
He knows the world over
    That Baby is king.

JOHNNY'S OPINION OF GRANDMOTHERS.

GRANDMOTHERS are very nice folks;
    They beat all the aunts in creation;
They let a chap do as he likes,
    And don't worry about education.

I'm sure I can't see it at all,
    What a poor feller ever could do
For apples and pennies and cakes
    Without a grandmother or two.

Grandmothers speak softly to "ma's"
    To let a boy have a good time;
Sometimes they will whisper, 'tis true,
    T'other way when a boy wants to climb.

Grandmothers have muffins for tea,
    And pies, a whole row, in the cellar,
And they're apt (if they know it in time)
    To make chicken-pies for a feller.

And if he is bad now and then,
    And makes a great racketing noise,
They only look over their specs
    And say, "Ah, these boys will be boys!

"Life is only so short at the best;
    Let the children be happy to-day."
Then they look for a while at the sky,
    And the hills that are far, far away.

Quite often, as twilight comes on,
    Grandmothers sing hymns very low
To themselves as they rock by the fire,
    About heaven, and when they shall go.

And then a boy stopping to think
    Will find a hot tear in his eye,
To know what must come at the last,
    For grandmothers all have to die.

I wish they could stay here and pray,
    For a boy needs their prayers ev'ry night;
Some boys more than others, I s'pose;
    Such fellers as me need a sight.

KITTY'S CAT AND MINE.

KITTY's cat has fresh blue ribbon
    Knotted on its throat of snow;
Mine has but a dingy fragment,
    Though I love the creature so.

Kitty's cat has sunny corners,
  Woolly rugs where she may lie;
But no sunshine lights my window,
  Nor a carpet soft have I.

Kitty's cat has dainty messes,
  Food and drink, without a care;
My poor Tricksy lives by mousing
  Up and down and everywhere.

Kitty's self wears pretty dresses,
  Lives a careless lady fine—
Might, like gorgeous Cleopatra,
  Drink up jewels in her wine.

I grow weary, stitching always—
  Always, for my life, you see;
Attic-room and counted cinders
  Make up all of life to me—

Except for Tricksy. Can you wonder
  I am glad at night to know
Something—I should say somebody—
  Waits for me, and tells me so?

So I bear no grudge to Kitty
  For the sunshine she has kept,
While about me, closing darker,
  Shadows still have closer crept.

But—I wish I had a ribbon,
  Quarts of milk, and woolly mat
For old Tricksy; so I'm jealous,
  After all, of Kitty's cat.

CRADLE AND GRAVE.

March 16, 1856.

AROUND a cradle courtiers bent
  Wherein a babe slept royally
Beneath the purple robe of state,
  Gemmed thick with 'broidered golden bee.

That tiny rosy palm held fast
  The slender link of empire's chain,
On which hung many a waiting hope
  Of dynasty enthroned again.

Kisses of welcome met its breath,
  A happy mother's blessing fell
From pallid lips above the child,
  Whose birth-cry stilled a fun'ral knell,

Whilst cannon thundered out the news,
  Flags bloomed like flowers in the air,
And down the brilliant avenues
  Re-echoed vivas ev'rywhere.

June 1, 1879.

Above poor Louis' last low couch
  Only the tangled grasses bent,
As though in pity for the lad
  So early from Life's battle sent.

No vivas woke that tropic air;
  Only the mouths of wounds agape

Told all the solemn story o'er
   Of ambush, combat, and mishap.

No loving kisses on the cheek,
   No mother's breath the soft air stirred;
His last good-bye the angels keep,
   For only they that message heard.

No cannon boomed to tell the news,
   No banner flung its shifting shade;
An empire slipped from out the hand
   Low on the tangled grasses laid.

"The prince is dead! the empire falls!"
   What matter? Still the world goes on;
But when we read "At Chiselhurst
   A widow mourns her only son,"

Then ev'rywhere throb mother-hearts,
   As Rachel's grief they understand,
And pray for her whose darling fell
   Asleep unkissed in Zulu-land.

EXPLANATORY NOTES.

Page 13.—ALL QUIET ALONG THE POTOMAC.—In the fall of 1861 "All Quiet along the Potomac" was the familiar heading of all war-despatches. So when this poem appeared in the columns of *Harper's Weekly*, Nov. 30th, it was quickly republished in almost every journal in the land. As it bore only the initials E. B., the poem soon became a nameless waif, and was attributed to various pens.

The *London Times* copied it as having been written by a Confederate soldier and found in his pocket after death. (It seems to have been a dangerous thing to copy it, as it has so often been found in dead men's pockets.) An American paper quoted it, saying that it was written by a private soldier in the United States service, and sent home to his wife. This statement was met by another, asserting that it was written by Fitz-James O'Brien. As the soul of that true poet and gallant soldier had gone out through a ragged battle-rift won at Ball's Bluff, this was uncontradicted until an editorial paragraph appeared in *Harper's Weekly*, July 4th, 1863, saying it had been written for that paper by a lady contributor.

It appeared in a volume of *War-Poetry of the South*, edited by Wm. Gilmore Sims, as a Southern production, and was set to music by a Richmond music-publisher in 1864, with "Words by Lamar Fontaine" on its title-page. A soldier-cousin, who went with Sherman to the sea, found in a deserted printing-office at Fayetteville a paper containing a two-column article on the poem, with all the circumstances under which "Lamar Fontaine composed it while on picket-duty."

It appeared in the earlier editions of *Bryant's Library of*

Poetry and Song over Mrs. Howland's name, which was afterward corrected by Mr. Bryant.

Within the last year a Mr. Thaddeus Oliver claims its authorship for his deceased father, being no doubt misled by a wrong date, as he fixes an earlier time than its first appearance in *Harper's Weekly*.

I have been at some pains to gather up these dates and names as one of the curiosities of newspaper-waif life. To those who know me, my simple assertion that I wrote the poem is sufficient, but to set right any who may care to know, I refer to the columns of the old ledger at Harper's, on whose pages I saw but the other day the business form of acceptance of, and payment for, "The Picket-Guard," among other contributions.

Fortunately, I have two credible witnesses to the time and circumstances of its writing. A lovely lady sitting opposite me at the boarding-house table looked up from her morning paper at breakfast-time to say, "All quiet along the Potomac, as usual," and I, taking up the next line, answered back, "Except a poor picket shot." After breakfast it still haunted me, and with my paper across the end of my sewing-machine I wrote the whole poem before noon, making but one change in copying it, reading it aloud to ask a boy's judgment in reference to two different endings, and adopting the one he chose. Nothing was ever more vivid or real to me than the pictures I had conjured up of the picket's lonely walk and swift summons, or the waiting wife and children. A short sojourn in Washington had made me quite familiar with the routine of war-time and soldier-life. The popularity of the poem was perhaps due more to the pathos of the subject than to any inherent quality.

Page 71.—GONE TO THE COUNTRY.—After three weeks of great physical suffering, which involved a thirst which must be denied, the school-boy went to the upper class. At first there were hopes that "going to the country" might be possible or beneficial, but when the pale lips answered, to some heavenly roll-call we who watched him might not hear, "I'm Willie

Stafford," we knew well the country whither he was bound. The verses were written at midnight in his lonely home, from which the silent sleeper and sorrowing parents had gone to lay him on the hillside "in the country."

Page 82.—WHICH SHALL IT BE?—This is the original title under which the poem appeared in the *New York Ledger*. Copied without name or credit given, it appeared elsewhere with a new title, "Not One to Spare," an explanatory and unauthorized foot-note added. In this form it drifted into the fine collection of poems made by Mr. Henry T. Coates under the title *Fireside Encyclopædia of Poetry*, and appears duly credited in the later editions of that beautiful volume.

Page 111.—FROST-SMITTEN.—*The Republican*, Goshen, N. Y.: "Died at his residence in this village, Sept. 21st, 1863, Judge Horace W. Eliot, aged 82."

Page 256.—JOHN ELIOT.—This poem was written for the gathering of the descendants of John Eliot, the Indian Apostle, at Guilford, Sept. 16th 1875,—the first that had ever taken place. Notices had been sent out all over the Union, and about two hundred "Eliots" assembled at the Guilford Point House, bringing heirlooms, old books and pictures, medals, and needlework of "ye olden time."

Page 261.—HYMN.—Written to be sung by the Eliot descendants in commemoration of the landing at Boston, Nov. 14th, 1631, of the good ship "Lyon," bearing, among sixty others, John Eliot. It is adapted to the tunes in use in colonial times, such as "Windsor," known in Scotland as "Dundee," the "Ten Commandment" tune, and "Old Hundredth."

Page 321.—RE-UNITED.—Three weeks before the death of Mrs. Robert Bonner a daughter died in her girlhood. At the large gathering of friends at the funeral in Dr. Hall's church one might fancy the fair silent figure in its last repose was carven marble, with the small hands so meekly folded on the stirless breast, like some mediæval saint. When so soon the shadow stooped again to lift the pale invalid mother up higher, one could not fail to think of that happy meeting above.

Page 317.—OFF BARNEGAT.—In the early morning of an intensely cold day in February the three-masted schooner David N. Tolck went on the bar, and there remained until she broke up. The child was taken safely ashore in the arms of the first mate, who was drawn in a canvas chair along the line connecting ship and shore. The small boats had broken up long before. While lashed to the mast the captain's wife sang hymns until death chilled her lips. The captain, somewhat infirm in health, seems to have died very soon, as the pair were found silent in death, the wife's head resting on his breast. The little orphan escaped quite safe from harm, and found kind hands to minister to her on shore.

www.ingramcontent.com/pod-product-compliance
Lightning Source LLC
Chambersburg PA
CBHW030303240426
43673CB00040B/1044